DATE DUE

JOSHUA PILCHER

JOSHUA PILCHER
Fur Trader and Indian Agent

JOHN E. SUNDER

UNIVERSITY OF OKLAHOMA PRESS
NORMAN

BY JOHN E. SUNDER

Published by the University of Oklahoma Press
Bill Sublette, Mountain Man (1959)
The Fur Trade on the Upper Missouri (1965)
Joshua Pilcher: Fur Trader and Indian Agent (1968)

LIBRARY OF CONGRESS CATALOG CARD NUMBER: 68–15680

Copyright 1968 by the University of Oklahoma Press, Publishing Division of the University. Composed and printed at Norman, Oklahoma, U.S.A., by the University of Oklahoma Press. First edition.

To My Mother

THIS IS A CANDID PREFACE, in keeping with Joshua Pilcher's character and with the tradition of the "honest preface," set by that great plainsman, the late Walter Prescott Webb, at The University of Texas in Austin, where I practice Western History.

I have a poor memory for middle initials and correct titles and dare not attempt to thank every archivist and librarian who helped me piece together this biography. Instead, I shall stand on safer ground and thank a few friends, with names I remember, who serve in institutions where most of this material came from: Mrs. Frances Stadler and Mrs. Lenore Harrington of the Missouri Historical Society in St. Louis; Miss Mary Louise Nelson and Miss Kathleen Blow of the University of Texas library; and Miss Jane F. Smith of the National Archives.

Since fur traders and Indian agents are not good subjects for research grants, I compiled Joshua Pilcher's life without asking for foundation support, other than some microfilm money granted by the University of Texas, and I typed the manuscript myself to avoid proofreading a typist.

To quote Webb out of context—he wouldn't mind—prefaces should "wink at each other in passing" and "never make a fuss."

Austin, Texas   JOHN E. SUNDER
March 20, 1968

CONTENTS

ix

JOSHUA PILCHER

To AVOID EXCESSIVE REPETITION, the following abbreviations have been used in the footnotes and in some entries in the bibliography. Full bibliographical information for books cited in the notes is given in the bibliography, pages 175–90.

Chouteau MSS: Chouteau Family Papers

Clark MSS: Clark (William) Papers

CtY-WA: Yale University, Western Americana Collection, New Haven, Connecticut

HBCo: Hudson's Bay Company Archives, Beaver House, London

HD: House Document

HED: House Executive Document

HR: House Report

KHi: Kansas Historical Society, Topeka, Kansas

LB: Letter Book

LR: Letters Received

LS: Letters Sent

Lucas MSS: Lucas Family Papers

MnHi: Minnesota Historical Society, St. Paul, Minnesota

MoHi: State Historical Society of Missouri, Columbia, Missouri

MoSHi: Missouri Historical Society, St. Louis, Missouri

NA: National Archives, Washington, D.C.

NHi: New-York Historical Society, New York City

OIA: Office (Bureau) of Indian Affairs

PAC: Public Archives of Canada, Ottawa, Ontario

RG: Record Group

RICC: Records of the Indian Claims Commission (Warehouse No. 3, Alexandria, Virginia)

SD: Senate Document

Sec. A, USGAO: Second Auditor's Office, Records of the United States General Accounting Office

TSLA: Tennessee State Library and Archives, Nashville, Tennessee

CULPEPER, THE BLUEGRASS,
AND THE CUMBERLAND

LATE IN MARCH, 1790, tax assessor Daniel Brown, a harbinger of
spring in the piedmont, rode the trails linking the isolated
farms along the runs of the Hazel and Thornton rivers west of
the Rappahannock. Brown's tax district, the northern half of
Culpeper County, Virginia, extended from near tidewater across
gently rolling red loam hills through thick hardwood and ever-
green forests to the front of the Blue Ridge. His long circuitous
route through sparsely populated country was dangerous in un-
predictable spring weather, but he knew the trails and had ridden
the hills many times to compile the tax rolls.[1]

At the end of a busy week in the backwoods he dismounted at
the home of an old friend, Joshua Pilcher, a forty-one-year-old
native of Culpeper County. Pilcher supported his wife, Nancy,
and eight children by farming a small tract of rented land. The
older children, Shadrach, twenty-two, Fielding, a year younger,
and Moses and Margaret, both in their teens, worked the farm
with their parents and helped provide for the younger children,
Benjamin and Zachariah, both under eleven, John, who was barely
two, and Joshua, the two-week-old baby, born on March 15.[2]

The Pilchers of Culpeper County were descendants of Robert

[1] Personal Property Tax List for 1790, Culpeper County, Virginia, on deposit
at the Virginia State Library, Richmond.

[2] For Joshua's date of birth see Directions given by Joshua Pilcher, May 29,
1843, respecting his lot in the Episcopal Cemetery and of his interment there,
St. Louis Courthouse Papers, MoSHi. Nancy Pilcher's maiden name and place
and date of birth cannot be located. She may have been Joshua Sr.'s second wife.
Joshua Sr. was born in 1749, Shadrach on February 27, 1768, and Margaret in
1777. The ages of the other children are approximate ones estimated from
census, tax, and genealogical records.

Pilcher, one of four brothers who emigrated from Wales to Maryland early in the eighteenth century. From Maryland Robert moved to Stafford County, Virginia, near the lower Rappahannock, then ascended the river to settle on the piedmont frontier. His son James married Phoebe Fielding and fathered Joshua.[3] Life was hard for the Pilchers in the Virginia hills; Joshua worked from sunup to sundown raising grain, tobacco, cattle, and hogs. When Daniel Brown visited the little Pilcher plantation in 1790 he assessed taxes on only two horses since Joshua's other personal property was too meager to be taxed.[4]

Each year Joshua plowed and planted his Culpeper farm, but reaped little for his effort and fell gradually into debt. Creditors sued him in the county court at least four times in four years and won the suits. To raise money he pledged everything he owned, yet some of his creditors still were unsatisfied.[5] His wife and older children knew there was no ready cash, but the young John and Joshua lived in a world close to their mother's apron strings, and would remember little of the family's hard early years in Virginia.

Debts and the daily struggle to make a living on a hill country farm forced the Pilchers to abandon Culpeper County in 1793. Daniel Brown had stopped by the farm on April 2 and may have discussed with them the Pilcher plan for leaving Virginia.[6] Preferring not to stay where his creditors hounded him, where his

[3] Genealogical information on the Pilcher family may be found in Margaret Campbell Pilcher, *Historical Sketches of the Campbell, Pilcher and Kindred Families*, and in Lewis S. Pilcher, *A Surgical Pilgrim's Progress*. Mrs. Margaret P. Vaughan, of Alexandria, Virginia, has compiled extensive genealogical notes on the Pilcher family.

[4] Personal Property Tax Lists for 1787–93, Culpeper County, Virginia, on deposit at the Virginia State Library, Richmond; Deed Record Book Q, pp. 118–19, Culpeper County Clerk's Office, Culpeper, Virginia.

[5] Deed Record Book Q, pp. 118–19, Culpeper County Clerk's Office, Culpeper, Virginia; Execution Book, 1790–94, *ibid*.

[6] Personal Property Tax List for 1793, Culpeper County, Virginia, on deposit at the Virginia State Library, Richmond.

children would grow up as illiterate as their parents, and where only propertied men held the right to vote, Joshua had decided to take his family across the mountains to start life over again in the new state of Kentucky, a promised land, some said, where the climate was temperate, good land was abundant, and the forests were filled with game to feed a man and his family until he brought in a crop. Shadrach and Fielding, the oldest Pilcher boys, may have gone to Kentucky a year or two earlier, taking some of the livestock with them.[7]

When the grass along the trails was high enough to nourish livestock, Nancy Pilcher packed a few parcels of food, clothing, and utensils; Joshua mounted the younger boys on a horse; and driving along a milch cow or two and a few hogs, the family headed west, probably over Swift Run Gap in the Blue Ridge and down into the Shenandoah Valley to the settlement at Rocktown (Harrisonburg). At Rocktown the family turned southwest on the Great Valley Road, ascending gradually the Shenandoah Valley. In company with hundreds of families bound for Kentucky and Tennessee, they traveled safely and easily through the long, fertile trough between the mountains, went through the road junction market town of Staunton, past tiny Lexington and Hans Meadow (Christiansburg). They saw the extraordinary natural bridge over Cedar Creek, at Radford they crossed the divide between the waters flowing to the Atlantic and those flowing to the Ohio, and they floated or forded the New River at Ingles' Ferry.

Beyond New River the road turned almost due west through wilder, less populated country surrounding old Fort Chiswell and the new settlement at Evansham (Wytheville). Thirty miles west of Abingdon, 280 miles from home, they reached the blockhouse near the Holston River where the Wilderness Road, a rough bridle path unsuited to wagons, wound west, whenever possible

[7] *Ibid.*, 1790–93; Pilcher, *Historical Sketches*, 367.

following stream beds over rocks, bogs, and fallen timber up and over Cumberland Gap into Kentucky. Moving frequently in parties, joined for companionship and protection against Indians and white outlaws, travelers on foot or on horseback filled the twenty-year-old trail. As many as 30,000 emigrants a year crossed the Gap going west, and until the Indian menace was removed from the Ohio country, the Wilderness Road was Kentucky's lifeline to Virginia.[8]

East of Cumberland Gap the road west from the blockhouse followed a tortuous, scenic route over or around successive mountain ranges, crossed fords of the Holston and Clinch rivers, and finally dropped into Martin's Station, in Powell Valley, the last dot of civilization on the map for 120 miles. Suddenly, from the base of Pinnacle Mountain, just west of the station, the travelers saw the outline of the gap etched against the western sky and started the short, steep ascent through a ravine leading to the top of the grand pass. On the Kentucky side of the gap the trail crossed rough mountainous terrain before dipping to a ford of the Cumberland River. Northwest of the ford it meandered through foothills to the bluegrass country and terminated, for all practical purposes, at Crab Orchard in Lincoln County.

Rapid travelers took seven days to pass through the wilderness between the blockhouse and the bluegrass. The Pilcher family, encumbered with small children, baggage, and stock, probably took longer. Since rain made portions of the road impassable and turned shallow river crossings into roaring torrents, they traveled as the weather permitted, took time to hunt game, and watched

---

[8] William A. Pusey, *The Wilderness Road to Kentucky*, Chaps. IV and V. Supplementary material appears in the following volumes, not cited in the bibliography: Archer Butler Hulbert, *Boone's Wilderness Road* (Cleveland, 1903); Robert L. Kincaid, *The Wilderness Road* (Indianapolis and New York, 1947); and in Thomas Speed, *The Wilderness Road* (Filson Club Publications, Vol. 2; Louisville, 1886).

carefully for Indian sign. Near Hazel Patch, in the foothills of the Cumberlands, they left the main road and followed Boone's old trail north to the beautiful valley of the Kentucky River and then —the town of Lexington, 500 miles from Culpeper County.

Lexington was the trade, social, and intellectual nucleus of Kentucky or, as some said, an exotic flower blooming at the end of a long stem rooted in Virginia and North Carolina. The town, containing perhaps three or four hundred homes, clustered around the courthouse, stood "in the midst of a vast plain as open as that of Philadelphia."[9] Not a major market, the community was a "[great] place for dealing": smiths, shoemakers, and hatters turned out quality goods, and a local brewer supplied the taverns.[10] Some good land was for sale near Lexington for seven shillings, about $1.20, per acre, much too high a price for Joshua Pilcher's thin purse.[11] Fortunately, he was not planning to buy a farm, but to rent, if he could find them, a few rich well-watered acres in Fayette County near Lexington, where he could see his children grow up and enjoy the advantages of a new life in Kentucky.

He looked for land carefully and shrewdly until the summer of 1795. He then arranged to share crop a tract south of town, below the road linking Lexington to Frankfort on the west and to Clark Courthouse (Winchester) on the east.[12] No farm was easy to work when fields had to be turned with a crude homemade wooden plow, harrowed with brush, and harvested by hand, but the family made a living by growing corn and perhaps hemp and tobacco.

[9] Victor Collot, *A Journey in North America* (trans. by J. Christian Bay), 102–103.

[10] "The Journal of Needham Parry—1794," *The Register of the Kentucky State Historical Society*, Vol. XXXIV (October, 1936), 382.

[11] Harry Toulmin, *The Western Country in 1793* (ed. by Marion Tinling and Godfrey Davies), 23.

[12] A. C. Quisenberry (ed.), " 'Heads of Families' in Fayette County, Census of 1810," *The Register of the Kentucky State Historical Society*, Vol. XX (May, 1922), 145, 158.

Beginning in 1796, Joshua paid taxes on twice as much livestock as he had owned in Virginia and, in 1804, he paid taxes for a slave.[13] There were only a few large slaveholders in Fayette County; most residents held no slaves or less than three. Certainly the Pilchers lived better in Kentucky than they had in Virginia, even if their daily diet probably varied little from the standard fat pork, corn bread, coffee, and mush.

In Kentucky the older Pilcher children exchanged life on the family farm for marriage and homes of their own. Shadrach and Moses lived alternately in neighboring Fayette and Jessamine counties; Fielding became a lieutenant in the Kentucky militia and moved to Woodford County west of Fayette; Margaret married Hiram Shaw, a merchant-hatter, and resided in Lexington.[14] Most of the Pilcher children, possibly all of them, learned to read and write. Although Kentucky had not started a public school system, a number of teachers in Lexington conducted classes for tuition-paying students in the three R's, bookkeeping, the classics, and music. Young Joshua may have attended one or more of these classes or he may have learned his letters from his older brothers; only wealthy families hired private tutors or sent their children to select academies. Whatever the source of Joshua's primary education, he learned to write clear concise sentences and to keep detailed complicated accounts.[15]

Joshua's boyhood days in Fayette County were filled with the sights and sounds of his three worlds: the farm where he worked in the fields, tended the stock, and did his chores; the nearby

[13] Tax Lists, 1796–1809, Fayette County, Kentucky, on deposit at the Kentucky Historical Society, Frankfort.

[14] Ibid., 1796–99; G. Glenn Clift, The "Corn Stalk" Militia of Kentucky 1792–1811, 109; G. Glenn Clift, Second Census of Kentucky—1800, 231; Ralph Shaw Typescript on the Shaw-Pilcher Families, p. 4, MoSHi; Pilcher, Historical Sketches, 367.

[15] Charles R. Staples, The History of Pioneer Lexington (Kentucky) 1779–1806, 297–303; Thomas D. Clark, A History of Kentucky, 303–307.

canebrakes and the forests of walnut, oak, maple, and sycamore, where he roamed and played; and cosmopolitan Lexington, within a few miles ride of home, where a young fellow sampled life in other ways. By 1802, blocks of substantial brick buildings dominated the center of Lexington, although the broad streets were unpaved. The tanyards that bordered the little spring-fed stream running through town, and other local industries—ropewalks, powder mills, print shops, and potteries—needed skilled labor, but the supply was short: a fact for a young man to remember if he should decide to leave the farm.[16]

About the time Kentucky first sent Henry Clay to the United States Senate, in 1806, Joshua moved into Lexington to become an apprentice hatter under his brother-in-law Hiram Shaw, who ran a hatter's shop on the corner of Main and Broadway.[17] The five or six hatters in Lexington employed dozens of assistants and produced annually $30,000 worth of fashionable wool and fur hats made of "beaver, muskrat and raccoon skins of superior quality."[18] Within a few years Joshua had learned the hatter's trade and the ways of the town.

During his years as an apprentice in Lexington the regional demand for Kentucky-made products grew because of the high cost of imported manufactured goods. Old enough to understand some of the political arguments he heard and read about, Joshua learned of the need for improving Kentucky roads and waterways to link Lexington's thriving market with the outside world, and he realized the necessity of protecting the state's infant industries against competition from the outside. However, he probably found

[16] François A. Michaux, *Travels to the West of the Alleghany Mountains, in the States of Ohio, Kentucky, and Tennessee*, 199–202.

[17] Ralph Shaw Typescript on the Shaw-Pilcher Families, p. 4, MoSHi.

[18] Staples, *Pioneer Lexington*, 253–54, 256; F. Cuming, *Sketches of a Tour Through the States of Ohio and Kentucky*, 186. See also such advertisements as those carried in the Lexington *Kentucky Gazette*, November 7, 1799, and *Independent Gazetteer*, March 8, 1805.

town life and the companionship of young ladies more diverting than politics. From Hiram Shaw's shop he could see Main Street crowded with carriages and some of the finest horses in the blue-grass; he could walk two blocks and watch the crowded courts in session in the new three-story brick courthouse; he could shop in the noisy marketplace; and, if he wished, at the end of the day he could meet other young apprentices and clerks at a coffee-house—one of which subscribed to over forty newspapers—or could spend his time at a tavern or a billiard parlor.[19]

His later familiarity with the art of medicine suggests that he may have studied medicine in his free time, although there is no documentary evidence that he ever practiced it professionally. The medical division of Transylvania University, in Lexington, was not organized until 1819, when Joshua lived in St. Louis, and his name does not appear in the early nineteenth-century lists of students who attended the institution. Since few American universities offered medical courses at that time many young doctors were trained directly by older physicians, and a young man like Joshua could read medicine with a doctor in Lexington, attend an occasional university lecture at Transylvania, and prepare himself for a medical career. A few of the doctors who practiced in Lexington before the War of 1812 were reputable physicians. Some, such as Dr. James Overton who kept "his shop on Main Street, nearly opposite to the court house," doubled as apothecaries and sold surgical instruments; some were quacks or transients who ran brief advertisements in the newspapers and then moved on.[20]

Lexington offered serious students advantages for study seldom found in a town of its size. Travelers were impressed by the "brick College" and theater, and remarked upon the two bookstores doing

[19] Cuming, *Sketches*, 182–88; Theodore G. Gronert, "Trade in the Blue-Grass Region, 1810–1820," *Mississippi Valley Historical Review*, Vol. V (December, 1918), 315–18.

[20] Staples, *Pioneer Lexington*, 318–24; *Reporter* (Lexington, Kentucky), October 21, 1809.

business in 1810 and the "circulating library containing about two thousand volumes where a person, at small expense, can have the perusal of almost any work."[21] Certainly, Joshua had access to medical books in Lexington either in the library, in bookstores, or in private collections. Moreover, his familiarity with smallpox prevention through inoculation—knowledge that he later put to use in the Indian country—may date from his years in Lexington, when both newspapers and doctors campaigned against the dread disease.

In the spring of 1810, Joshua celebrated his twentieth birthday and presumably began to think about his future. Both the "clean and well fenced; gently undulating" fields of Fayette County and the brick and "neatly painted" frame homes of Lexington looked familiar to him after seventeen years of residence there. He felt as much at home in the muddy marketplace square, where the pillory and stocks stood, as he did on the farm.[22] Many of his fellow Kentuckians shared his liberal religious and republican political ideas, the community was prosperous—land close to town sold for $200 an acre, and little good land was left in the country under $12.00 an acre—and he could depend upon relatives and friends to help him in business or a profession. Perhaps he would stay in Lexington.[23]

Then, in mid-summer 1810, his "aged and infirm" father died. By a provision in his father's will, dated May 3, Joshua inherited a four-year-old brown horse. The Pilcher household was broken up—the crops, stock, furniture, and utensils were sold—and Nancy Pilcher moved in with one of her married children late in

[21] John E. Bradford (ed.), "The James McBride Manuscripts," *Quarterly Publication of the Historical and Philosophical Society of Ohio*, Vol. V (January–March, 1910), 24–25.

[22] Alexander B. Grosart (ed.), *The Poems and Literary Prose of Alexander Wilson, the American Ornithologist*, I, 191–93.

[23] John Melish, *Travels Through The United States of America, in the Years 1806 & 1807, and 1809, 1810, & 1811*, 404.

1810 or early the following year. Joshua, free to leave Kentucky if he wished, mulled over the problem during the winter, and decided to ride south as soon as the roads were passable.[24] Twenty-one was an appropriate age for a young man to break home ties and, as there is no proof of a better reason for his decision to abandon Kentucky, we may presume he responded to the urge to make his way, entirely on his own, in a new land.

Lexington was the hub of the Kentucky road system and a major point on the post road that swung west and then south in a wide arc to Tennessee. In 1811 the post road was the fastest and most direct route from the bluegrass plateau to middle Tennessee, the most likely route for Joshua to take to reach the Cumberland Valley, where the post road intersected a road running west through Gallatin to Nashville. Only one-third the size of Lexington, Nashville was rapidly becoming the political center of Tennessee, and the capital would be moved there from Knoxville in 1812. It supported three newspapers, a college, and a variety of small businesses. The speculators and the wealthy planters who owned the best land in the valley traded in Nashville and wielded strong influence there.[25]

[24] Will Book B, February, 1809–October, 1813, pp. 152–53, Fayette County Court, Lexington, Kentucky; Order Book 2, April, 1808–October, 1811, pp. 279–80, *ibid.*; Executors Bonds No. 2, 1803–27, p. 77, *ibid.*; Quisenberry (ed.), " 'Heads of Families,' " *The Register of the Kentucky State Historical Society*, Vol. XX (May, 1922), 158. Nancy Pilcher's place and date of death are unknown. She may have remained in Kentucky to live with Fielding, Benjamin, or Margaret; she may have remarried; or she may have moved to Indiana, where her son Zachariah settled in the 1820's, or to Illinois with her son Shadrach. Moses died in 1806, and John in 1813. *Ed Pilcher* v. *Fielding Pilcher*, 1821, Metal File Box 523–525, Fayette County Court, Lexington, Kentucky; Fourth Census of the United States (1820), Fayette County, Kentucky, Records of the Bureau of the Census, RG 29, NA.; (Mrs.) William B. Ardery (comp.), *Kentucky Court and Other Records*, II, 21; Fifth and Sixth Census of the United States (1830 and 1840), Fayette County, Kentucky, Records of the Bureau of the Census, RG 29, NA.

[25] Thomas P. Abernethy, *From Frontier to Plantation in Tennessee*, 204–209.

Middle Mississippi Valley and Adjacent Areas, 1793–1843

Late in the spring Joshua rode through innumerable cotton and tobacco fields beside the narrow, dark blue Cumberland, then jogged up a road to the top of the high bluff on which Nashville perched above the valley. The usual public buildings, post office, jail, courthouse, and market-house, dominated the center of town. Private homes lined the narrow unpaved streets leading to the square or clung like so many birds' nests to the edges of the bluff.[26] Joshua probably stopped at one of the inns near the square while he looked over locations for a hatter's shop and examined the furs, from the Ohio Valley and Great Lakes, available on the Nashville market. The streets, especially on market days, were crowded with potential customers for hats: small farmers from the backwoods, mechanics, merchants, and planters. But his capital was limited and he had to invest it carefully.

He negotiated with a merchant named John Lowry, perhaps the same Lowry who formerly had been a prominent dealer in furs and hats in Lexington, and bought his "interest in the Hat Store at Nashville." Lowry ran a newspaper advertisement beginning July 7 requesting "all those endebted [to him] to make payment to Mr. Joshua Pilcher," and Joshua announced, in a note to the advertisement, that the "business will be continued at the same house . . . where will be on hand a supply of Hats, of the best quality." He did not buy the lot and building occupied by the store nor did he purchase any other land during his residence in Nashville, always preferring, it seems, to rent rather than buy real property.[27] This was a fortunate decision because during the winter of 1811–12 major earthquakes rocked the Ohio and Mississippi valleys, and in Nashville, to the expense and dismay of property owners, "chimneys were thrown down, scaffolding

[26] Anne Royall, *Letters From Alabama on Various Subjects*, 19.

[27] *Democratic Clarion & Tennessee Gazette* (Nashville), September 24, 1811.

around many new buildings fell with a loud crash," and walls cracked.[28]

Joshua earned a comfortable living as a Nashville merchant-craftsman. When war with Britain started in June, 1812, he chose to remain in Nashville rather than return to Kentucky to enlist, as did his brother Shadrach, his nephews, and his cousins, or leave with the Tennessee volunteers mobilized by Andrew Jackson and the young lawyer-politician Thomas Hart Benton for defense of the southwestern frontier.[29] Colonel Benton of the Second Infantry Regiment of the Tennessee Volunteers passed through Nashville several times during the war years and may have met Joshua at that time. Later, in St. Louis, they would become fast friends; Joshua would grow to be fond of Benton's son John Randolph and his daughter Jessie, who would marry the controversial army officer and future presidential candidate John Charles Frémont. Frémont's father taught French, cavalry tactics, and broadsword techniques in Nashville during the war, and Joshua could have known both father and son there at that time.[30]

Joshua's last two years in Nashville were his most eventful ones in Tennessee. In 1813 he joined eighty leading citizens who petitioned the state assembly to control the "numerous Tipling Shops erected on the high way and in our Towns by free Negroes and others" who violated the Sabbath, sold stolen whiskey, and encouraged drunkenness. Servants and slaves were lured into the roadside drinking dens, and some citizens feared that a slave conspiracy might hatch in the "sinks of corruption." The assembly tabled the petition, and the "Tipling Shops" remained open.[31]

[28] Samuel C. Williams, "Nashville As Seen By Travelers, 1801–1821," *Tennessee Historical Magazine*, Series II, Vol. I (April, 1931), 196–97; William Henry McRaven, *Nashville, "Athens of the South,"* 67–68.

[29] Tax List, 1811–12, Davidson County, Tennessee, on deposit at TSLA.

[30] *Nashville Whig*, September 7, 1813.

[31] Petition to the General Assembly from Citizens of Davidson County Re-

On the evening of March 2, 1814, fire broke out in Anthony Foster's home on the square and spread quickly to a neighboring office and an adjacent brick home. A strong northwest wind blew firebrands over most of the town, and at least twenty buildings caught fire before the conflagration was extinguished. Two children burned to death, and property damage was estimated at twenty to thirty thousand dollars. Joshua lost his stock in the fire and suspended business for a month until he could rent "a small brick building near to where he formerly lived, on market street" and reopen his shop.[32]

Shortly before the fire, Cumberland Lodge No. 8 of the Masonic Order had been chartered in Nashville. Joshua joined the Lodge, received the Past Master's degree, and then petitioned and was admitted to membership in the Grand Lodge of Tennessee—all within a few months. Since only Master Masons received the Past Master's degree and qualified to join a Grand Lodge, Joshua must have participated in Masonry before he associated with the order in Nashville, yet no record exists of his earlier Masonic activity. At the "communication of the grand Lodge of the State of Tennessee," held in Nashville early in October, 1814, he represented Cumberland Lodge No. 8 and served as Grand Junior Deacon of the meeting.[33]

Three weeks after the annual convocation of the Grand Lodge he announced that he was closing his shop in Nashville and called upon his customers to settle their accounts.[34] The fire and, perhaps, the wartime shortage of raw materials and labor to make hats had

---

specting Negroes and Tipling Shops, 1813, Petitions and Memorials, Tenth General Assembly of the State of Tennessee, TSLA.

[32] *Nashville Whig*, April 6, 1814. For details on the fire see *ibid.*, March 8, 1814 and April 18, 1815, and the *Clarion & Tennessee State Gazette* (Nashville), March 8, 1814.

[33] *Clarion & Tennessee State Gazette* (Nashville), August 30, 1814; Charles A. Snodgrass, *The History of Freemasonry in Tennessee 1789–1943*, 31, 33.

[34] *Nashville Whig*, October 25, 1814.

apparently discouraged him. He seems to have had more cash on hand late in 1814 than he had three years earlier when he left Kentucky. Still single, he could pack his saddlebags and ride the road to opportunity wherever it led, and now it led to Missouri.

Missouri Territory was new and largely undeveloped, but like the rest of the Mississippi Valley it was a logical choice to draw thousands of settlers and enjoy unmatched prosperity once the war was over. St. Louis, in the center of the valley near the junction of the Missouri and Mississippi rivers, seemed to be the best place for an ambitious, talented young man to settle and wait for the war to end and for prosperity to begin. Unfortunately for Joshua, St. Louis was nearly three hundred miles due northwest of Nashville, and could be reached only by difficult roundabout routes that connected the two towns. The long and dangerous Natchez Trace ran southwest from middle Tennessee to Natchez, on the Mississippi River, where travelers had to wait for poor, intermittent water transportation upriver to St. Louis. But interconnecting post roads leading from Tennessee across Kentucky into southern Illinois Territory provided a shorter, more direct route to St. Louis—the route he probably took late in the fall of 1814.

S⊤. LOUIS, capital of Missouri Territory, was an unimpressive
town of less than three thousand inhabitants. As Joshua
stepped from the ferry at the town's edge, he saw a jumble of
stone and whitewashed buildings and smelled the litter piled in
the three streets paralleling the river. The rolling countryside that
stretched west beyond the town looked far more appealing than
the sandy levee on which the town was built. American occupation
of the Louisiana country west of the Mississippi, a decade earlier,
had had little effect on the characteristic Gallic life of St. Louis,
but by 1814 the Americans were altering, subtly but surely, the
appearance and culture of the settlement. Within another seven
years postwar migration would double the population, the French
role in politics would diminish—practically evaporate—and gamb-
ling, duels, and brawls would become commonplace in the rapidly
changing community.

The war still was under way when Joshua reached the Territory,
and St. Louis was almost encircled by hostile Indians, who killed
settlers within a few miles of town and drove frontier farmers to
shelter in crude timbered blockhouses. Travel north and west of
St. Louis was particularly risky. The Indian trade had recoiled
from the back country for the duration, and 350 mounted
Missouri militiamen, under General Henry Dodge, were fighting
tribes in western Missouri, but the war with Great Britain was
nearly over. On Christmas Eve, 1814, peace commissioners signed
the Treaty of Ghent ending the conflict; two weeks later Andrew
Jackson, unaware of the treaty, defeated the British in the post-
treaty Battle of New Orleans.

Peace returned to Missouri in the spring of 1815. In spite of

unsettled Indian problems on the Mississippi, river trade reopened, merchants inventoried their stock for the postwar market,
and Joshua invested his capital in a business partnership with N. S.
Anderson. Pilcher and Anderson sold dry goods, rented storage
space to other merchants, and may have dealt in a wide variety of
general merchandise.[1] The partnership lasted approximately a
year, until Anderson died in the summer of 1816. In August,
Joshua and Anderson's executor dissolved the business and called
in all unpaid accounts. Presumably, most of "those indebted to the
said concern" settled their accounts quickly, although Joshua had
to sue at least one customer for an unpaid bill.[2]

His partner's unexpected death left him without adequate
capital. Perhaps if Anderson had lived another five years, Joshua
could have carried on in business alone; as it was, he needed a new
partner. He chose an older fellow-Virginian, Thomas F. Riddick,
or, as seems more likely, Riddick, an influential merchant, politician, and banker who had lived in St. Louis ten or twelve years,
chose Joshua. His wife, Eliza Carr Riddick of Lexington, Kentucky, may have known the Pilcher family when Joshua was a
young apprentice hatter. The Riddicks and their four children
became Joshua's closest friends in St. Louis, and he frequently
enjoyed the hospitality of their home.[3]

In November, 1816, Riddick and Pilcher opened a downtown
auction business with ample storage space in "a new frame warehouse" at the rear of their office.[4] The warehouse was so con-

---

[1] Bill of Chouteau to Pilcher & Anderson, March 3, 1816, Chouteau MSS,
MoSHi; *Missouri Gazette* (St. Louis), May 25, 1816; Edgar B. Wesley, "Diary
of James Kennerly 1823–1826," *Missouri Historical Society Collections*, Vol. VI
(October, 1928), 64 (n. 74).

[2] *Missouri Gazette* (St. Louis), August 17, 1816; *Joshua Pilcher* v. *Joshua
Norvell*, 1821–22, Metal File Box 529–531, Howard County Circuit Court,
Fayette, Missouri.

[3] Frederic L. Billon, *Annals of St. Louis in its Territorial Days From 1804
to 1821*, 188–89.

[4] *Ibid.*, 138. The Riddick-Pilcher partnership probably dated from as early

veniently located that the Bank of Saint Louis rented space there temporarily in December, 1816, and Christ Church, the first Protestant Episcopal congregation organized west of the Mississippi, was founded there three years later.[5] Scores of new brick buildings were under construction in St. Louis and, despite high prices for food, rent, labor, and raw materials, Joshua profited in the auction business with Riddick during the postwar good times when settlers by the thousands poured into the Mississippi Valley.[6]

The Masons, having failed twice to organize permanent lodges in Missouri, in the prewar period, succeeded after the war. The Grand Lodge of Tennessee issued a dispensation on October 3, 1815, directing Joshua, Thomas Brady, a merchant, and Joshua Norvell, a Nashville newspaperman, to organize a Missouri lodge. In the fall of 1816, at the time Joshua formed his partnership with Riddick, Missouri Lodge No. 12, later renamed Missouri Lodge No. 1, was chartered in St. Louis. Joshua was named First or Charter Master; Brady, Senior Warden; and Jeremiah Conner, a prominent Irish politician, Junior Warden. Eliza Riddick's brother, William C. Carr, was elected secretary of the Lodge, and a few years later Riddick served as Grand Master of the Grand Lodge of Missouri.[7]

At first the lodge met in two rooms on the second floor of a brick store near the Riddick and Pilcher auction house, but the crowded meeting place was unsuited generally to Masonic procedure. Accordingly, they pressured the territorial assembly, sitting down the street, to allow them to raise at least $8,000 to build

as September. See Estate of Edmond Shipp, File No. 252, St. Louis Probate Court, St. Louis, Missouri.

[5] Marietta Jennings, *A Pioneer Merchant of St. Louis 1810–1820*, 172.

[6] Solon J. Buck (ed.), "Pioneer Letters of Gershom Flagg," *Transactions of the Illinois State Historical Society For the Year 1910*, 152–53.

[7] James B. Steiner, *History of Missouri Lodge No. 1*, 5–18, 58–59, 62–63, 87; William R. Denslow, *10,000 Famous Freemasons*, III, 342; *Missouri Grand Lodge Bulletin*, Vol. IV (November, 1927), 167.

a lodge hall. In January, 1817, the assembly passed legislation appointing Joshua and four lodge brothers to conduct a fund-raising lottery. Thousands of tickets were sold at the Riddick-Pilcher store and other business houses scattered about town and, when the money had been raised, brother Thompson Douglass was commissioned to add a third-floor Masonic meeting hall to his new two-story brick store. He added the third story immediately, and the lodge moved in before the end of the year.[8]

Personal relationships between lodge members were not always fraternal, even in 1817. Joshua and a fellow Mason, young Stephen F. Austin, then a member of the Missouri Territorial Assembly and later founder of the first American settlement in Texas, quarreled over a young lady. The two men may have known each other in Lexington before 1810 when Austin was a student at Transylvania. Suffice to say, in mid-May, 1817, when the Masonic lottery was under way in St. Louis, Austin called upon Joshua to learn why his "once esteemed" friend was treating him coldly. Joshua answered by letter and received an immediate lengthy letter in reply from Austin who vowed that he was "unconscious of ever haveing [sic] at any time, in any place or under any circumstances injured you or wounded your feelings or even harboured the Most distant the least Shadow of an intention to do so in my life."

Joshua charged, however, that Austin had repeated to others a story he had told him, in strict "Masonic confidence," about his broken engagement with a girl in Nashville. Austin swore that he had heard the story from acquaintances first, but that after Joshua had told him the story he held it to be confidential. According to Austin, Joshua believed Austin intended to compete for the affec-

---

[8] L. C. Dyer, "The Early Days of Freemasonry in Missouri," *The Missouri Freemason*, September 27, 1913; *Missouri Gazette* (St. Louis), March 22, 1817; *Acts Passed By The General Assembly Of The Territory of Missouri; In December and January, One Thousand Eight Hundred and Sixteen and Seventeen*, 64.

tions of a certain "Miss F." of St. Louis. Austin denied that he planned to court the young lady, although he had recently walked her home from a play to which Joshua had escorted her and bought her ticket. Suspicious of Austin's conduct, although he said he "never [permitted] suspicions to govern [him] . . . I am always govern'd by existing fact," Joshua gave in to his hot temper and assaulted Austin on the street, badly injuring one of his eyes.

For at least ten days Austin was incapacitated by his eye injury, and unable to demand immediate satisfaction of Joshua. A duel on Bloody Island in the river near St. Louis seemed inevitable under the sensational, widely discussed circumstances. The Masons, shocked by the impending fight, called the two men before the lodge for an explanation—Austin appeared, but Joshua sent his friend Thompson Douglass as his spokesman—and appointed a three-man committee "to watch the Hostile movements of said Brothers against each other." On June 1, Austin formally challenged Joshua to a duel, ignoring the fact that dueling was "equally abhorrent to Religious Masonry and Law." At that point Joshua, surprisingly, held his temper, allowing a Masonic committee of four to examine the disagreement. A week later they reported that Austin "never did intentionally give cause of offence to Mr. Pilcher" and that "Mr P's coolness arose from mistaken impressions." They recommended that Joshua write Austin to apologize for the attack and injury and to admit that he acted under incorrect impressions. Later in the day Joshua wrote the apology, but no more, and the trivial issue that had led to a serious confrontation was settled.[9]

A few months later his friend Benton, who had moved to St. Louis after the war, fought a duel with young Charles Lucas, the

---

[9] The quotations appear in the documents relating to the duel compiled by Eugene C. Barker (ed.), *The Austin Papers*, II, 306–15. See also P. M. Newmill, "Stephen F. Austin, Duelist," *Bunker's Magazine*, Vol. I (January, 1928), 47–56.

son of a powerful political adversary. They met on Bloody Island on a hot, muggy September day and exchanged shots simultaneously. Lucas died in the presence of seconds and surgeons. St. Louisans heard that Joshua witnessed the bloody affair, but the evidence contradicts the rumor. Two of Benton's three better biographers state that Joshua was not present on the island. Perhaps he wasn't there that day, but he was always Benton's loyal political supporter: Benton's friends and enemies were his friends and enemies, and would be until the day he died.[10]

In Missouri, as in most American territories created in the western wilderness beyond the original colonies, personalities were more important than parties in determining political strength and weakness. What and who a man was was indicated by which faction he belonged to and which ones he opposed. This was particularly important in the so-called "Era of Good Feeling" after the war when the Democratic-Republican party ruled supreme and, on the surface at least, all politicians fluttered in the same coop. In Missouri one faction of the great national party included many wealthy French landholders and Indian traders allied to Governor William Clark, territorial delegate John Scott, and Benton. Another powerful faction formed around the Lucas family and such officeholders as Rufus Easton and David Barton. The two groups, neither of which held broad-based popular support, struggled for power in the territory until the great quarrel over slavery and statehood shuffled the antagonists into two new stacks.

Although Joshua probably adhered to the Creole-Clark "little junto," as Joseph Charless, editor of the *Missouri Gazette*, called it, he devoted more time to trade than to politics after the war.

10 Statement of Witnesses to the Lucas-Benton Duel, September 27, 1817, Lucas MSS, MoSHi; *Missouri Gazette* (St. Louis), October 4, 11, November 1, 15, 1817; William M. Meigs, *The Life of Thomas Hart Benton*, 112; William N. Chambers, *Old Bullion Benton*, 72–76; Elbert B. Smith, *Magnificent Missourian: The Life of Thomas Hart Benton*, 63.

Business partnerships, at that time, were highly personal, flexible, and frequently only verbal agreements that allowed the partners to participate in other businesses. Although Joshua worked long hours in the auction house with Riddick—clerks and junior partners oftentimes put in a twelve- to fourteen-hour day—he found time to take an interest in other enterprises.[11]

The mines at Potosi and Mine à Breton, in the Ozark foothills, supplied lead for the lead-processing industry at Herculaneum twenty-five miles south of St. Louis. Both Stephen Austin's father and Riddick's half-brother, like many other Missourians, invested in the new river town. Joshua visited Herculaneum at least once before he quarreled with Austin and may have ventured some capital in the lead mills, wharves, or shot towers that were notable landmarks in the community.[12] Otherwise, "most of the houses were built of squared oak logs, and had bulky old fashioned chimneys, built outside with a kind of castelated air."[13]

Joshua was also interested in banking and participated wholeheartedly in the complicated affairs of the Bank of Saint Louis, which was chartered by the territorial legislature in 1813. His partner, Riddick, was one of the original bank commissioners who struggled nearly four years to raise sufficient capital ($150,000) to open the bank. Although most businessmen favored the institution and there was no other bank in St. Louis, the stock was subscribed fitfully because trade was slow during the war and many merchants had no experience in dealing with banks. Barter, instead of cash, was still an important means of local trade, and debts were seldom paid on time. But when the bank first opened on December 13, 1816, in the Riddick-Pilcher warehouse, postwar prosperity

[11] Lewis E. Atherton, *The Pioneer Merchant in Mid-America*, 10, 42, 88.

[12] Barker (ed.), *Austin Papers*, II, 309; Jennings, *Pioneer Merchant*, 81–82, 87.

[13] Henry R. Schoolcraft, *The Indian in His Wigwam*, 30.

assured it good business, and it soon moved into a renovated stone building close by.[14]

Poor management combined with land speculation pushed the bank into trouble almost immediately. On February 11, 1818, Joshua, by then a director, charged at a meeting of the board that the cashier was responsible for issuing excess notes and introduced a resolution, "offered for . . . four weeks successively," to remove the cashier. Joshua, a hard-money man who stood by notes redeemable in specie, spoke for the more conservative stockholders. After the board complied with his request and fired the cashier, Joshua moved that the board select a new one, but the man chosen was unacceptable to Joshua and two other directors, Elias Rector and Robert Simpson. They resigned in protest and, supposedly, threatened to close the bank at once. The board declared their seats vacant and adjourned, touching off what was later termed a "tumultuous assemblage" of stockholders and others outside the bank.[15]

The crowd, or mob, as some "moral & religious" St. Louisans who shuddered "at such outragious [*sic*] proceedings" called it, entered the bank, led by Joshua, Benton, and several other stockholders and directors, and resolved "to possess themselves of the keys of the outer door."[16] The bank clerks gave them the keys and scurried away while the angry group locked the doors and withdrew to the Riddick-Pilcher store where they demanded that the bank president give them the keys to the vault. He refused. They then set up a five-man committee to protect their interests as stockholders and to keep everyone out of the bank until the board agreed to their demands. But the board refused to turn over the

[14] John Ray Cable, *The Bank of the State of Missouri*, 47–52.

[15] *Ibid.*, 54–55; Jennings, *Pioneer Merchant*, 172; Chambers, *Benton*, 78; Billon, *Annals*, 87; *Missouri Gazette* (St. Louis), February 20, March 13, 1818.

[16] E. B. Clemson to John B. C. Lucas, February 14, 1818, Lucas MSS, MoSHi; *Missouri Gazette* (St. Louis), February 20, 1818.

vault keys or to discuss bank policy with the rebellious faction, and fearing "great bodily harm," asked the United States Circuit Court to indict Joshua and his friends for taking over the bank. On February 13 the grand jury returned "not a true bill," yet the court bound Joshua and ten others in bonds of $1,000 each to keep the peace for six months.[17] Joshua explained later that the "tumultuous assemblage . . . spoken of in the protest" of the bank board to the court "did not happen to be half so large as it is every day in the week, of honest peaceable citizens who attend Col. Riddick's auctions . . . and who perhaps knew no more of what was going on in the Bank opposite, than if they had been on the Rocky mountains."[18] Nevertheless, he was under a peace warrant and had to curb his impetuousness.

On February 16 the insurgents returned the keys of the outer door to the directors, who announced, within a few hours, that the institution would reopen on February 23. Joshua agreed that the delay "was a good one, that it required time for the new Cashier . . . to ascertain and know something of the situation of the Bank," but he became furious when he saw a new notice delaying opening until March 10.[19] The board charged that "a combination [had] been formed for the purpose of embarrassing" the bank. Joshua and his associates protested their innocence and issued a countercharge: the bank refused to redeem its notes in specie, yet was "receiving payments from many individuals who are obliged to enter the Banking House by a private door."[20] In a lengthy letter, published in the *Missouri Gazette*, Joshua asked if the bank would ever reopen.

Under pressure from disgruntled stockholders, the bank reopened in mid-March with a reorganized board of directors. They

[17] *Missouri Gazette* (St. Louis), February 20, 1818; Record 1, 1816–19, pp. 148, 150, St. Louis Circuit Court, St. Louis, Missouri.

[18] *Missouri Gazette* (St. Louis), March 13, 1818.

[19] *Ibid.*

[20] *Ibid.*, March 6, 1818.

resumed specie payment but failed to strengthen the bank adequately, and after sixteen months of uncertainty closed the business permanently in the summer of 1819. Meanwhile, the newly chartered Bank of Missouri had opened, backed by several powerful French families who needed a friendly bank to support their investment in the fur trade north and west of St. Louis. The Bank of Saint Louis had not co-operated with them; the Bank of Missouri would. Riddick, Benton, and probably Joshua, allied themselves to the new institution.[21]

During the spring and summer of 1819, while the Bank of Saint Louis was dying, Joshua crossed the great divide in his career—from merchandising and banking to the fur trade. Business in St. Louis was still good: new homes were going up in the city; sawmills hummed; billiard rooms, dance halls, the theater, and the markethouse were crowded; carts jammed the unkept streets. Affluent citizens wore stylish clothes, furnished their homes tastefully, and assembled private libraries.[22] Nevertheless, the boom was dissolving in a wave of recession. Joshua was nearly thirty, not quite a young man by the standard of those times, and his decision to begin a new career probably was not an easy one to make. Riddick, an honest businessman, a man of integrity and influence, was his partner, and Joshua had made money in the auction house, but, at the same time, he had made enemies in St. Louis. Some of his associates pictured him as an ill-tempered street brawler and leader of mobs. Others believed him to be simply an excitable man of strong loyalties and beliefs. Few could deny that he was ambitious and energetic, a hard-worker, and a driving force in any organization to which he belonged.

He knew something about the fur trade, but little about the

---

[21] *Ibid.*, March 13, April 24, 1818; Cable, *Bank of Missouri*, 56–60.

[22] LeRoy R. Hafen and Harlin M. Fuller, *The Journal of Captain John R. Bell*, 55–61; Ferdinand Ernst, "Travels In Illinois In 1819," *Transactions of the Illinois State Historical Society for the Year 1903*, 154.

Indian country. In Lexington and Nashville he had learned to distinguish good quality fur from poor and how to turn raw fur into finished hats. In St. Louis he had become familiar with fur storage, the techniques of fur auction, and the banking problems of the fur business. From his business associates and Masonic brothers who had invested in the fur trade he had learned the general structure of the industry. Yet his knowledge of the western Indian country was limited to what he read in the newspapers, observed in such places as Governor Clark's council room filled with Indian artifacts and natural history curiosities, heard from hunters and travelers passing through town, or learned from keelboatmen on the levee.[23] Nonetheless, his character well suited him for any job that demanded imaginative leadership, and in the summer or early fall or 1819, he joined the Missouri Fur Company.

The original St. Louis (Missouri) Fur Company had been organized in 1808–1809 by the Creole trader Manuel Lisa and a handful of investors. Lisa, a New Orleans merchant who had settled in St. Louis in the 1790's had found trade regulations cumbersome before the United States purchased Louisiana from France. In 1807, after the purchase, he began to realize his dream by leading a trading expedition to the Yellowstone country. Within five years he had laid the foundation of a vast trading empire on the upper Missouri River, maintained by permanent trading posts and parties of roving traders. By competing successfully with British traders from Canada, he had helped strengthen the American position in the Northwest. Although the company had been reorganized periodically, Lisa remained its leader and planner.[24]

During the War of 1812 he gave up his foothold in the dangerous Dakota border country and concentrated his trade at

<hr>

[23] James Haley White, "Early Days in St. Louis," *Glimpses of the Past*, Vol. VI (January–March, 1939), 6.

[24] Walter B. Douglas, *Manuel Lisa* (ed. by Abraham P. Nasatir), 391.

Council Bluffs. When the war ended, he slowly expanded his domain upriver once again, aided by legislation forbidding British fur companies from operating on American soil and by the Convention of 1818 which defined the border between the United States and Canada as far west as the Continental Divide. Postwar prosperity, expanding fur markets, and the increasing activity of the United States army along the Missouri encouraged him to organize a new Missouri Fur Company in 1819. The new association was in reality a four-year partnership of vigorous young men directed by the older and more experienced Lisa.

Lisa held six of the thirty shares in the company, his brother-in-law Thomas Hempstead, Andrew Woods, Joseph Perkins, one of Joshua's Masonic brothers, and Joshua himself each subscribed to four shares. Kit Carson's brother Moses B. Carson (another Mason) and John B. Zenoni took two shares apiece. The remaining four shares were alotted later.[25] Joshua may have purchased a portion of his shares with capital he borrowed on a business trip to New Orleans and Havana in the spring of 1819.[26] His investment in the Missouri Fur Company was a great risk since the fur trade was a gamble at best, and Lisa was nearly fifty years old, but if the company could push the Indian trade closer to the Rockies and the headwaters of the Missouri, as Lisa planned to do, they might turn a handsome profit.

Before the winter of 1819–20 settled over the Missouri Valley, Lisa returned to his post, Fort Lisa, at Council Bluffs, accompanied by his wife, her female companion, and several other traders, including Joshua. The Lisas settled at the fort until spring, but Joshua moved from Indian camp to Indian camp trading for furs

[25] Richard E. Oglesby, *Manuel Lisa and the Opening of the Missouri Fur Trade*, 172–73; Dale L. Morgan (ed.), *The West of William H. Ashley*, L.

[26] (Mrs.) Dana O. Jensen, "The Enigma of Mr. Shaw," *The Bulletin of the Missouri Historical Society*, Vol. XV (July, 1959), 311; *Joshua Pilcher v. William Grayson*, 1819, Metal File Box 176, Howard County Circuit Court, Fayette, Missouri.

during the unusually bitter winter, learning the rudiments of the business. In December he and an army lieutenant from nearby Cantonment Missouri (later Fort Atkinson) made a circuit of approximately 250 miles across the treeless, ravine-cut plains of eastern Nebraska to visit the Omaha Indians. Joshua bartered for 130 beaver pelts plus deer and raccoon skins and returned to Council Bluffs in time to participate in the exchange of Christmas greetings between the Fort Lisa traders and the army men from the Cantonment.[27]

Lisa's health deteriorated during the winter at Council Bluffs, and Joshua assumed more authority at the post. When the Missouri River was ice-free, in late March, the Lisas began to pack and early in April left for St. Louis. When Lisa reached Franklin, Missouri, on April 16, he discussed company business with partners Woods and Perkins. A few days later he landed in St. Louis.[28] Joshua remained at Council Bluffs during the spring, absorbing details of the fur trade and observing the Indians. He formed close friendships with John Dougherty, Indian interpreter at Council Bluffs, who accompanied him on at least one of his visits to the Indians in the fall of 1819, and with young and handsome William Henry Vanderburgh. In time business and politics destroyed Joshua's friendship with Dougherty, but Vanderburgh and Joshua remained cordial until the younger man's untimely death in 1832.[29]

Lisa's health worsened in St. Louis during the spring and summer of 1820. Finally, under the care of a physician, he moved to a

[27] Edwin James, *Account of an Expedition from Pittsburgh to the Rocky Mountains, Performed in the Years 1819, 1820*, 269.

[28] Joseph Perkins to Joshua Pilcher, April 17, 1820, Fur Trade Papers, MoSHi.

[29] Margaret Stauf, "John Dougherty, Indian Agent," *Mid-America*, Vol. XVI (January, 1934), 139; Paul C. Phillips, "William Henry Vanderburgh: Fur Trader," *Mississippi Valley Historical Review*, Vol. XXX (December, 1943), 379.

suburban watering place, but found little relief at the mineral springs. Meanwhile, Joshua had returned to St. Louis and was hard at work running the company. One of his first duties was to investigate the theft of furs from the company warehouse. On August 2 he appeared before a justice of the peace to arrange the commitment of James Watts for stealing beaver skins.[30] Joshua was no stranger to trouble; it simply made him more determined to stand his ground. His money and his career were tied up in the Missouri Fur Company; if the company had to fight in court to hold itself together, he was willing to fight. He had gone to court three times since 1819, and was about to go again to untie the knots left from his earlier partnerships with Anderson and Riddick. Legal tangles were not new to him.[31]

Early in the morning of August 12, Lisa died quietly. In his will, signed a few hours before, he empowered his executors "if necessary" to mortgage his property in St. Louis "to secure a debt to Messrs Stone Bostwick & Co for goods purchased for the . . . Missouri Fur Company." Lisa hoped that his partners would persevere in the fur trade, despite supply problems, losses to the Indians, and larceny in St. Louis.[32]

[30] Commitment of James Watts, August 2, 1820, Lucas MSS, MoSHi; *Thomas Hempstead, Joshua Pilcher et al surviving partners* v. *G. H. Robb*, Case Papers No. 7, October Term, 1822, Fur Trade Papers, MoSHi; Deposition of Michael Immell, June 25, 1821, in Charles E. Peterson, "Manuel Lisa's Warehouse," *The Bulletin of the Missouri Historical Society*, Vol. IV (January, 1948), 78.

[31] Circuit Court Record No. 2, 1819–23, pp. 59, 62, 67, 125, 132, 244, 293, 346, 530, Howard County Circuit Court, Fayette, Missouri; *Joshua Pilcher* v. *Thompson Douglass*, Case Papers No. 182, August Term, 1819, St. Louis Circuit Court, St. Louis, Missouri; *Missouri Intelligencer* (Franklin), February 4, 1820.

[32] Thomas Hempstead to Joshua Pilcher, May 15, 1820, Hempstead Papers, MnHi; Manuel Lisa's will quoted in Oglesby, *Manuel Lisa*, 177–78.

31

STRONG, shifting political winds blew through the streets of St. Louis in the summer of 1820, to swirl about the heirs of Manuel Lisa and the directors of the Missouri Fur Company. In mid-June delegates met at the Mansion House to write a state constitution authorized by a recent Congressional enabling act. Influenced directly by the Missouri Compromise, they drew up a slave-state constitution and presented it to Congress without first submitting it to a popular referendum in Missouri. Riddick sat as a proslave delegate to the convention, and Joshua shared his sympathies. Two weeks after Lisa's death the voters elected a state administration. When the assembly convened in September a majority of the legislators agreed that David Barton should hold one of the seats in the United States Senate, but argued bitterly over the other seat before choosing Benton to fill it. Once in the Senate, Benton fought for the interests of the private fur companies against the publicly owned fur factories created by the Federalists late in Washington's administration. Although the factories did not operate northwest of Missouri, the possibility that they might be extended farther west threatened the private traders who fought against the factories and lobbied to destroy them. In the spring of 1822, Benton would fire the coup de grâce that would kill the system and satisfy Joshua and many other fur traders.

The death of the factory system, less than a year after Missouri entered the Union in August, 1821, stimulated the flow of capital into the western fur trade, but international events were as important as money to the rejuvenation of the trade. As a result of the Anglo-American Convention of 1818 that had placed the Oregon country west of the Continental Divide under joint occupation, American fur traders had renewed efforts to penetrate the land beyond the headwaters of the Missouri. Then in 1819, Spain, in the Adams-Onís Treaty with the United States, had relinquished its old claim to Oregon and defined the irregular borderline between the Louisiana Purchase and the Spanish Southwest. A few years later Russia would, in separate treaties with Great Britain and the United States, step back from Oregon, and the entire area between the crest of the Rockies and the Pacific Ocean from the forty-second parallel north to the Alaskan panhandle would be free of all but British and American influence. By then the Hudson's Bay Company would have absorbed the North West Company, thus presenting a united front to American fur trade competitors in the Northwest. The Missouri Fur Company watched the changing situation in Oregon closely and worked to build "a chain of posts from the western limits of the State of Missouri, across the country, to the Pacific Ocean."[1]

Immediately after Lisa's death the company shareholders had drawn up a new four-year partnership agreement to begin on September 20, 1820. At once Joshua had set out for Council Bluffs to oversee the company's upriver trade during the coming winter while Thomas Hempstead remained in St. Louis to serve as business manager. He had acted in that capacity for the partnership since 1819 and was one of the executors of Lisa's estate. His job as caretaker of the Lisa estate was not a simple one, but he moved easily amongst the men Joshua disliked, the "ruffled shirts gentry" of St. Louis, and took company trouble in stride.[2] Some of the other partners manned tiny, poorly protected trading stations

---

[1] "Joshua Pilcher's Report" of December 1, 1831 in "Message from the President of the United States, In Compliance with a Resolution of the Senate concerning the Fur Trade, and Inland Trade to Mexico," 22 Cong., 1 sess., SD No. 90, pp. 12–13.

[2] Thomas Hempstead to Joshua Pilcher, September 11, 1821, Thomas Hempstead LB (Missouri Fur Company), 1821–23, CtY-WA; Oglesby, Manuel Lisa, Chap. VII. For details of the questionable business practices of Stone, Bostwick &

along the Missouri that were easy targets for Indian attack. In April, 1820, a large Arikara war party had robbed two Missouri Fur Company posts near the Big Bend of the Missouri and had "beat and abused the men in charge of the houses."[3] Such attacks were common; they might happen at any time, at any post.

Although Hempstead lived securely and comfortably in St. Louis, his duties as company bookkeeper and purchasing agent were constantly frustrating. The market for robes and furs was unstable—it fell in the fall of 1820—debts piled up periodically, and the partners shared their grievances with him at every opportunity. Trade goods reached St. Louis late or not at all, despite protests to Oliver Bostwick, who represented the partnership's principal supplier, Stone, Bostwick and Company. As competition in the fur trade increased, particularly in 1822, keelboats to carry goods upriver from St. Louis to Council Bluffs became increasingly hard to find, credit became more and more expensive, and reliable fur traders, when available, commanded larger salaries. When debts forced Mrs. Lisa to offer to sell her stock in the company, Hempstead feared the shares would be bought by someone who would disrupt company policies.

By the end of September, 1820, Joshua was at Council Bluffs, where he passed the winter formulating plans for the spring trade. Since the furs gathered by the company in 1820 were insufficient to pay for goods advanced them that year, Joshua preferred to wait at Fort Lisa before pushing upriver, while Hempstead negotiated for goods from Stone, Bostwick and Company, hoping that fur prices might increase, especially on the European market. During the winter, Joshua sent men to build Cedar Fort (Fort Recovery), a small post protected by cottonwood pickets, a cannon,

---

Company see Richard E. Oglesby, "The Fur Trade as Business," in John F. McDermott (ed.), *The Frontier Re-examined*, 121–25.

[3] "Mr. Pilcher's Answers to questions put to him by the Committee of the Senate on Indian Affairs," March 18, 1824, 18 Cong., 1 sess., *SD No. 56*.

and diagonal towers, on an island in the Missouri River just north of the mouth of the White. The fort was needed to give their traders a protected jumping-off place to the upper Missouri. Disappointed because the army had failed to place a fort on the Yellowstone as a buffer against the British, Joshua was determined to push upriver, if necessary without military support.[4]

Spring brought good news—fur prices were up and trade goods prices down—and bad news—Hempstead did not have supplies to ship on time. In February he sent whiskey, tobacco, and a few other indispensable items, but it was late in July before he loaded a keelboat with most of the merchandise that Joshua had expected in the spring. The goods were barely stowed aboard when someone cut the mooring, or it parted, and the craft was adrift. Hempstead's men retrieved it undamaged several miles downstream, and the boat was headed upriver into the Missouri. Near Fort Bellefontaine, sabotaged by someone aboard, or so the circumstantial evidence indicated, it sank in the dark early hours of August 13, taking the entire cargo with it. Within a month Hempstead purchased and sent another boatload of merchandise to Fort Lisa. Two hundred miles below Council Bluffs floating ice halted it for the winter. In December when he packed barley, corn, and beads overland to Council Bluffs, Hempstead found it there. Joshua, "dangerously ill" in October, had recovered sufficiently by then to help Hempstead rescue the men and supplies beached downriver from Fort Lisa. Then, early in 1822, they packed the supplies overland, possibly by sleigh and two-wheeled cart, to the outlying company posts.[5]

---

[4] Thomas Hempstead to Joshua Pilcher, September 15, 1820, Fur Trade Papers, MoSHi; David Lavender, *Bent's Fort*, 31; Paul C. Phillips, *The Fur Trade*, II, 393.

[5] Thomas Hempstead to Joshua Pilcher, February 19, 1821, Fur Trade Papers, MoSHi; Joshua Pilcher to Ramsay Crooks, June 16, 1822, Chouteau MSS, *ibid.*; Thomas Hempstead to Joshua Pilcher, August 13, 1821, and to Oliver Bostwick, November 2, 1821, and January 1, 1822, Hempstead LB, CtY-WA.

Joshua had improvised supplies as best he could during most of 1821 and had stuck as closely as possible to his timetable for developing trade in the Northwest. Late in the summer two of his most dependable lieutenants, a St. Louisan, Robert Jones, and a large, muscular former infantry officer, Michael Immell, had reached Council Bluffs with approximately 180 men recruited in Missouri. Joshua immediately sent the men into the field. Under his orders they penetrated the Crow country, built a post, Fort Benton, on the south bank of the Yellowstone near the Big Horn junction, and traded with the Crows. In early fall Joshua wrote Hempstead that fur returns for 1821 were promising. Hempstead hoped for a large return, for enough furs and robes to "establish the credit and standing of the Missouri Fur Company to the great mortification of some people in [St. Louis]."[6]

In his first eighteen months as manager of the company in the field, credit and supply problems notwithstanding, Joshua had strengthened the partnership. Jones and Immell were working on the Yellowstone, feeling out the Crow trade before moving into the dangerous Blackfoot country around the headwaters of the Missouri and the upper tributaries of the Columbia. Joshua's plans for the Mandan trade were ready for the spring of 1822, and, with the army at least, the company reputation was high. General Henry Atkinson wrote Secretary of War John Calhoun from St. Louis late in November, 1821, "that the character of the trade has materially changed since the winter of 19–20, particularly as it relates to the Missouri Fur Company." Atkinson referred to Joshua's "integrity & uprightness of character," and his willingness "to promote the views of the agents of government in the discharge of his duties, as well as observing a strict conformity with the laws regulating intercourse with the Indians."[7]

[6] Thomas Hempstead to Oliver Bostwick, November 2, 1821, and to Joshua Pilcher, July 22, 1821, Hempstead LB, CtY-WA.

[7] Quoted in Morgan (ed.), *Ashley*, liv.

Every bit of praise, public or private, had helped to strengthen company credit in St. Louis and the East. A good business reputation was important, particularly in the spring of 1822 when Hempstead posted a $5,000 bond to renew the company trading license for the year, because new competitors were entering the trade and old ones were expanding operations.[8] Berthold, Chouteau and Pratte (the French Fur Company), who dominated the Indian trade in Missouri, ordered its men to compete vigorously with Joshua's traders, whenever possible, between Council Bluffs and the Mandan villages. Hastily they built Fort Lookout (Fort Kiowa) near Fort Recovery to fight Joshua for the Sioux trade. The $50,000 investment of the Missouri Fur Company in the fur trade was being threatened from still another side by a former lead miner and old Indian trader, Andrew Henry, and his new partner, William Henry Ashley, Missouri's Virginia-born lieutenant governor. Henry led a trapping party to the Yellowstone in 1822 and battled Jones and Immell for the Crow-Blackfoot trade. In St. Louis, Ashley competed with Hempstead for supplies and boats and recruited fur trappers, rather than traders, since he planned to substitute roving bands of trappers for the older system of traders and trading posts still used by the Missouri Fur Company and by Berthold, Chouteau and Pratte. The Ashley-Henry men, under contract as free trappers, not mere employees, would set their own beaver traps and no longer depend upon the Indians to bring them pelts.

In spite of greater competition, 1822 was a reasonably profitable year for the Missouri Fur Company. Joshua sent nearly three hundred traders into the field under Vanderburgh, Moses Carson, young and romantic Lucien Fontenelle, and a new company partner, Andrew Drips. Hempstead sent merchandise to Council Bluffs from St. Louis in time to supply the outlying posts before

[8] "An Abstract of All Licenses Granted by Superintendencies of Indian Trade, &c. &c.," 18 Cong., 1 sess., *HD No. 7*, p. 5.

winter set in, and the company accumulated approximately $42,000 in furs.[9] Joshua and Hempstead refused offers, from John Jacob Astor's righthand-man, Ramsay Crooks, to desert the Missouri Fur Company, and help Astor extend his Great Lakes fur empire as far as the Missouri River. Joshua wrote Crooks that he would stick by the Missouri Fur Company, at least until the partnership expired, when he hoped to extend the agreement and perhaps bring in "several young gentlemen who have been ingaged [sic] in the service of the Company," and who "look to me with confidence as a head as a leader." He asserted that he wished to end strife in the fur trade, but lashed at the "intriguing Creouls [sic] of the West possessing neither integrity spirit or enterprise, whether they be stationed at St. Louis or elsewhere."[10]

A few weeks after Joshua refused Crooks's offer he ascended the Missouri through the Sioux country—the Ashley-Henry trappers had gone upriver ahead of him—and stopped at the Arikara villages located a few miles south of the present North and South Dakota state line. He carried with him a temporary appointment as special Indian sub-agent, issued by Benjamin O'Fallon, United States Indian agent for the upper Missouri tribes. Joshua had "anticipated difficulties" with the Arikaras, who were also called the Rees, but they professed friendship and promised not to attack fur traders in the future. Although he was well acquainted with their "former [blood-thirsty] disposition," he gave them presents and wrote O'Fallon "a very favorable letter respecting them, and the prospect of their future good behavior." They parted as friends, and he continued upriver to the Mandan villages where he supervised construction of Fort Vanderburgh, named

[9] Thomas Hempstead to Joshua Pilcher, May 12, 1822, Hempstead LB, CtY-WA; Testimony of Michael E. Immell in *William Easdale* v. *Thomas Hempstead*, Case No. 71, April Term, 1821, Transcript from St. Louis Circuit Court in Manuel Lisa Papers, MoSHi.

[10] Joshua Pilcher to Ramsay Crooks, June 16, 1822, Chouteau MSS, MoSHi.

after his close friend. Twelve miles above the Knife, the new post tapped the Mandan-Hidatsa (Gros Ventre) trade and gave the company an important station between Fort Recovery and Fort Benton. If Fort Vanderburgh flourished, Joshua anticipated placing another post near the confluence of the Missouri and Marias.[11]

Late in the fall he realized that the Arikaras had deceived him. An Arikara chief, who had visited him in the Mandan country and learned when he planned to return to Council Bluffs, hid a war party along the river to attack Joshua's boat, as it floated down the Missouri from Fort Vanderburgh. The attack failed, but Joshua learned a valuable lesson about the Rees and was not surprised, although angered, when they later "attempted . . . to rob . . . and committed violence upon" one of his men. The Rees were a dirty dissolute agricultural tribe who liked the white man's trade goods yet disliked hunting beaver to trade for them. To solve the dilemma, they became middlemen between the fur traders and the western hunting tribes and struck out at all fur traders who threatened their position. Most traders despised the Rees—"the Horrid Tribe;" the "bete noir of the American trade"—and never turned the other cheek.[12]

Again, Joshua retired to Fort Lisa for the winter, his fourth in the Indian country. Hempstead brought up another supply caravan, paid Joshua a brief visit, and returned to St. Louis early in 1823 in wet, miserable weather. A month later he sent Joshua the details of conversations he had held with Berthold, Chouteau and Pratte over a possible co-partnership between the two trading firms. Hempstead's terms had been unacceptable to the Creole opposition, so he repaired his political fences and gathered supplies for the upriver posts. He estimated company credit in St. Louis as equal to or better than the credit of the other fur-trading groups, although he was upset because some indiscreet traders, and

[11] "Mr. Pilcher's Answers," March 18, 1824, 18 Cong., 1 sess., *SD No. 56.*
[12] *Ibid.*; Lewis O. Saum, *The Fur Trader and The Indian*, 47, 56.

even partners, talked and wrote too much to the wrong people about company business.[13]

When the snowdrifts melted and the streams ran high in the spring, Jones and Immell, who had wintered at Fort Benton, led their men west towards the Three Forks country under instructions "to obtain a friendly interview with the Blackfoot Indians . . . and to impress them with the friendly disposition of American citizens toward them." Andrew Henry was in the same field that spring looking for Blackfeet and for beaver pelts. He found the Blackfeet first and lost four men before he could retreat to his tiny stockade on the Yellowstone. Jones and Immell hunted up Jefferson's Fork of the Missouri without seeing any Blackfeet, but on the way back down the Jefferson thirty-eight turned up, led by a chief carrying a letter in English attesting to his good character. The traders and Indians camped together for the night, but Jones and Immell were suspicious of the Blackfeet and moved east, away from the Indians, "with all possible expedition" and caution when they broke camp in the morning. On May 31, near Pryor's Fork of the Yellowstone, a large Blackfoot war party ambushed them along a narrow trail; killed Jones, Immell, and five of their men; wounded four others; and stole their traps, pack horses, and pelts. The survivors fled across the Yellowstone to shelter in a Crow village.[14]

One member of the party, William Gordon, immediately carried news of the disaster to Fort Vanderburgh. There, on June 15, he wrote a letter to Joshua and handed the message to a company expressman who carried it downriver—the Rees fired on the ex-

[13] Thomas Hempstead to Joshua Pilcher, February 12, 1823, Hempstead LB, CtY-WA.

[14] "Mr. Pilcher's Answers," March 18, 1824, 18 Cong., 1 sess., *SD No. 56*; William Gordon to Joshua Pilcher, June 15, 1823, in Abraham P. Nasatir, "The International Significance of the Jones and Immell Massacre and of the Aricara Outbreak of 1823," *The Pacific Northwest Quarterly*, Vol. XXX (January, 1939), 100–101.

press canoe—to Joshua at Fort Recovery. Led by Charles Keemle, a Philadelphian who later became a journalist, the survivors of the ambush on the Yellowstone built skin canoes, loaded them with furs cached from the fall hunt, and floated down to join Gordon at the Mandan villages. Gordon blamed the Blackfoot attack on "the British traders, who have most probably instigated them to commit this outrage," and demanded that "something decisive should be done" about British trading posts on American soil.[15] Joshua also blamed the British traders, but at that moment could do nothing about them because he was involved in Arikara Indian troubles. Although there is no evidence that the British had provoked the attack, Hudson's Bay Company records reveal that the Blackfeet who ambushed Jones and Immell carried the stolen Missouri Fur Company pelts north to Edmonton Factory in Alberta.[16]

The loss of Jones and Immell—Joshua called them "the flower of my business"—and the loss of the pelts and equipment, valued at $15,000 to $16,000, staggered the Missouri Fur Company. Joshua was forced to pull his men back from the Northwest and to concentrate upon holding his trade together below the Mandans. He struggled for months to overcome the disaster on the Yellowstone, yet the company, short of capital and its credit jeopardized by the loss of the furs from the Blackfoot country, seemed to lose spirit. Hard work and vigorous management failed to restore public confidence in the company, and its traders never returned to the headwaters of the Missouri.

During the same summer the Arikara war was hurting company trade in the Dakotas. Late in May, on almost the same day that Jones and Immell fell on the Yellowstone, a trading party from St. Louis led by Ashley reached the Ree villages. Although

[15] Nasatir, "International Significance," *The Pacific Northwest Quarterly*, Vol. XXX (January, 1939), 101–102.

[16] *Ibid.*, 82–87.

the Indians seemed friendly, they were actually in no mood for peaceful trade but were seeking revenge for the loss of two men in a daylight attack on Fort Recovery several weeks earlier. "Their uniform hostility to Americans, and disposition to commit all sorts of depredations," Joshua remarked, influenced their relations with white men, as did their fear that if Ashley succeeded each year in sending trappers northwest of the Ree villages the Rees would lose out as middlemen in the fur trade.[17]

Since they found the Indians unexpectedly friendly, Ashley and his men tied up their two keelboats and landed at the Ree villages, and traded for pack horses and buffalo robes. As the weather was too wet and windy to allow them to move the horses, several of Ashley's men encamped on shore, below the villages, to guard the stock. During the night of June 1–2 one of the men from the camp stole into the lower Ree village and was killed. At dawn the Rees fired upon the traders holed up on the beach behind a weak barricade of sand and equipment. Traders and pack-horses dropped before the Ree fire, until finally, in great confusion, the survivors retreated into the water and swam for their lives, to the keelboats. Ashley counted his dead and wounded—twenty-four of them—and ordered the keelboats downstream where they halted briefly near a stand of timber. There, he transferred all the trade goods and wounded men to the larger boat and sent it down past the Sioux to Fort Atkinson, at Council Bluffs, carrying the news of the battle. In the smaller boat he and the other survivors dropped down the Missouri to the mouth of the Cheyenne River to await help.[18]

On June 18 the larger keelboat reached Fort Atkinson, and the men aboard delivered letters from Ashley to O'Fallon and Colonel Henry Leavenworth. O'Fallon favored immediate meas-

[17] "Mr. Pilcher's Answers," March 18, 1824, 18 Cong., 1 sess., *SD No. 56.*

[18] The best accounts of the Ree conflict are found in Dale L. Morgan, *Jedediah Smith and the Opening of the West*, Chaps. II and III, and in Morgan (ed.), *Ashley*, 24–56.

ures to chastise the Rees and, when he told Joshua of the attack on Ashley, Joshua wholeheartedly agreed with him. Colonel Leavenworth "could not doubt for a moment that it was [his] duty to move promptly and extend 'protection' to Genl. Ashley and to 'impress the Indians with our capacity to avenge the injury which they had done us.' "[19] He issued marching orders to six infantry companies and on June 22 set out by land and water for the upper river.

Joshua followed close behind with an army howitzer from Fort Atkinson and sixty men in two boats, which caught up with Leavenworth's keelboats on June 27. A few days later Joshua took aboard eleven barrels of provisions rescued from an army boat that had sunk. Leavenworth "highly appreciated" Joshua's willingness to transport the barrels free of charge until he could find space for them on another craft. They halted for four days, July 19–23, at Fort Recovery, where Joshua received the news of the death of Jones and Immell, and where he recruited Sioux auxiliaries to serve as Leavenworth's scouts. The Colonel liked Joshua. He was impressed with his efficient conduct and believed correctly that Joshua was "much better informed than myself" on Indian affairs.[20] At every opportunity Joshua and O'Fallon stressed, to Leavenworth, the importance of harsh action against all the Rees, not just punitive action against a few. On July 23, Joshua wrote O'Fallon: "If protection of the commerce of the Missouri be the object of our government . . . a decisive blow is indispensable for the safety of every white man on the river above

[19] "Leavenworth's Final and Detailed Report," October 20, 1823, reprinted in Doane Robinson (ed.), "Official Correspondence Pertaining to the Leavenworth Expedition of 1823 into South Dakota For the Conquest of the Ree Indians," *South Dakota Historical Collections*, Vol. I (1902). Unless noted specifically, the narrative and quotations on the Ree campaign are taken from this report, pages 203–33.
[20] Colonel Henry Leavenworth to Benjamin O'Fallon, July 21, 1823, *American State Papers*, II (Military Affairs), 589.

the Council Bluffs; and even to the troops stationed at that post." He believed that "the future conduct and disposition" of all the upriver tribes depended on the success of the Leavenworth expedition and predicted that the Rees would hold their ground at their villages. Brigadier General Henry Atkinson, commander of the Western Department of the army, thought the Rees would flee to the Mandan country, but Atkinson was wrong—the Rees resisted.[21]

Late in July the infantry under Leavenworth moved north from Fort Recovery and met Ashley near the Teton River. Joshua and some Sioux auxiliaries—old enemies of the Rees—encamped with Leavenworth and Ashley while they waited for additional Sioux warriors to join the expedition. Leavenworth organized everyone into the Missouri Legion under his command. He gave Joshua "the nominal rank of Major" in charge of an estimated 750 mounted warriors, and appointed Vanderburgh and Joshua's clerk, Angus McDonald—a Virginian, West Point graduate, and former army officer—nominal captains, and Moses Carson and William Gordon, nominal lieutenants, to lead forty traders, representing the Missouri Fur Company, in the expedition.

They broke camp early in August and moved upriver again. Two bands of Sioux hailed them from the riverbank on August 3 and invited them to a feast. Joshua and Leavenworth talked with Fire Heart, the Sioux chief, and invited the Indians to strike their lodges and join the expedition. They agreed, Leavenworth transported them across the river to the west bank, and the expedition proceeded upriver. On August 6 and 7 additional Sioux warriors joined them and were issued "powder and balls."

The following day most of the troops and traders landed south of Grand River. From there they marched north along the bank

[21] General Henry Atkinson to General Edwin P. Gaines, August 19, 1823, *ibid.*, 582; Joshua Pilcher to Benjamin O'Fallon, July 23, 1823, in Morgan (ed.), *Ashley*, 48–50.

of the Missouri to within a few miles of the Ree villages where, on the afternoon of August 9, Leavenworth sent Joshua and the Sioux ahead to keep the Rees occupied in the field while Ashley with the traders and the regular infantry moved into position. So far Leavenworth was "very well satisfied with Mr. Pilcher in every respect" and "highly appreciated" (one of the Colonel's favorite expressions) Joshua's willingness to take his boats and men north of Fort Recovery even though the Missouri Fur Company had lost almost its entire investment on the river above the Sioux country. However, Leavenworth distrusted Joshua's half-blood Sioux interpreter, Colin Campbell, and suspected that Campbell might do "all in his power to increase the influence and importance of [the Missouri Fur Company], not only at the expense of other traders but also at that of our expedition."

The Sioux dashed ahead towards the Ree villages faster than Leavenworth had anticipated. To slow their advance, he rode after them but found only Campbell. Joshua, apparently confused by the Colonel's orders, "had halted [most of] the Indians nearly a mile (and perhaps more) in the rear of the first line of advancing Indians." Leavenworth decided immediately not to rely upon the Sioux as his scouts and ordered them to guard the flanks, but the Sioux, probably urged on by Campbell, ignored Leavenworth's order, rode ahead of the advancing line of infantry and fur traders, and clashed with the Rees below the lower village. The Rees resisted stoutly and held their ground until the infantry and the traders drove them back behind the pickets of their villages. At dusk the keelboats carrying the army artillery reached the battle-field, but Leavenworth decided to wait until morning before launching a general attack on the villages. Unfortunately for the Colonel's reputation as a tactician, the assault by artillery and small arms on the following day failed. The villages held, and Leavenworth was uncertain what to do next.

The Sioux, however, were certain. They were hungry; they had dismembered and stripped the Rees they had killed in battle; and now, a bit bored by the white man's warfare, they looted the Ree corn, bean, and pumpkin patches. Some of the Sioux galloped away from the battlefield to sit on the sidelines while they waited to join the winners, whichever they might be. When Leavenworth's superiors heard later that the Sioux "deserted . . . at a critical moment, without giving any reason, and in a bad humor," they concluded that Indian auxiliaries were "not to be trusted, without a regular force of superior numbers sufficient to restrain and coerce them." Fearful that the Sioux might take advantage of the Arikara debacle to "commence a war with us," they urged that the Indians be watched "narrowly" in the future.[22]

Joshua faced a predicament on the battlefield. Since he was losing control of the Sioux and receiving highly contradictory battle reports from his men, he urged Leavenworth to take some decisive action that would encourage the Indian auxiliaries to remain in the battle. Not willing to take a bold step at this time, Leavenworth ordered his men to conserve ammunition, and warned the Sioux to leave the cornfields before the Rees could catch and kill them one by one. The Sioux, evidently insulted by the Colonel's message, pulled out of the Arikara country during the night. Late in the afternoon of August 10, Leavenworth and Joshua met a small party of Rees near the stockade of the lower village, and Leavenworth, to Joshua's disgust, told them he wished to make peace. But Leavenworth also was in a predicament that day: he was short of supplies; his attack on the two towns had failed; his Sioux allies were deserting him; he dreaded the cost of a long Indian campaign; and he was fighting a battle far from Fort Atkinson without specific orders from his superiors. Uncertain, he negotiated with the Rees.

[22] R. Lowndes order of General Gaines, September 21, 1823, and General Henry Atkinson to General Edwin P. Gaines, September 13, 1823, *American State Papers*, II (Military Affairs), 594–95.

The peace parley was held just outside the gates of the lower village shortly after Leavenworth and Joshua met the Rees near the stockade. As the peace pipe passed from chief to chief, officer to officer, Joshua's temper flared. At first he declined to smoke the calumet, then took a puff to humor Leavenworth, but refused to participate in the negotiations and warned the Rees " 'that War Chief [Leavenworth] has said you shall be safe, and you shall be so, But tomorrow I will speak to you.' " Since Campbell had told the Rees that Joshua "was the principal, or first chief of [the] expedition," the Indians were impressed by his wrath. As the council broke up, Leavenworth could hardly cope with Campbell's theatrics. The interpreter "kept his thumb on the cock of his rifle . . . snatched a pipe tomahawk from one of the Indians, and threw it in the rear," and threatened to kill one of the Rees. Several shots were fired—one ball grazed Joshua—and everyone scurried from the meeting place.

The following day, August 11, Leavenworth placed Campbell under guard, resumed talks with the Indians, and concluded a treaty he had to draw up himself because Joshua and Andrew Henry—who had descended the Missouri from the Yellowstone in time for the battle and was the only other Indian sub-agent at the council—refused to help draft the document. The Rees promised to return Ashley's property and to allow Americans to navigate the Missouri and pass through the Arikara country in peace. Joshua believed the agreement was worthless and said so: two important Ree chiefs had not signed, and Ree promises were empty, anyway.

Leavenworth and Ashley signed the treaty, but as Joshua had probably expected, the Rees restored only part of Ashley's equipment. Leavenworth held Joshua partially to blame for Ree unwillingness to "give up their horses to remunerate Gen.l Ashley," because the Indians feared they would need the horses to escape from Joshua and the Missouri Fur Company traders who "appeared to think that they were not bound by [the treaty]" and "had thrown their whole weight against [it]." While his men grew "anxious to charge upon the towns," Leavenworth waited until he could delay no longer—even Joshua favored delay on August 13—and then ordered battle resumed the following morning, August 14. Although the Rees had threatened to flee the villages during the night, Leavenworth thought they would stay because he had promised, at the last moment, not to press them to restore the remainder of Ashley's property. The villages were empty at dawn on the fourteenth, the Indians having slipped past Leavenworth's sentries during the night. The Colonel's scouts failed to find the Rees, and so, early on August 15, the infantry and the fur traders started downriver on the keelboats. Joshua's lieutenant, Angus McDonald stayed behind, and probably assisted by William Gordon, violated Leavenworth's orders and burned the villages.[23] Shocked by this action and annoyed by Joshua's conduct in the campaign, Leavenworth sent his superiors a lengthy report of the Ree expedition and added: "I regret to say that [Pilcher] appeared to be influenced by some secret and hidden cause, of which I had no knowledge, and to entertain very erroneous ideas as to my powers and duties, as well as his own."

Joshua denied responsibility for the fire, but were there "hidden causes," as Leavenworth stated, for his hostility to the treaty? No reliable proof exists that Joshua acted from ulterior motives, yet some of his critics were convinced that he was guilty of gross deception. The fullest summary of charges against him appears in a letter written at Fort Atkinson five months after the Arikara campaign by an important member of the expedition—possibly by Leavenworth himself—to a friend in St. Louis. The writer described Joshua as a man filled with "inveterate malice, without

---

[23] McDonald admitted he set the fire in a letter to the *Washington Gazette*, September 13, 1824, reprinted in part in Morgan (ed.), *Ashley*, 57. See also Colonel Henry Leavenworth to Major Alexander Macomb, December 20, 1823, in *ibid.*, 69.

the least regard to the truth," and wrote that, although Joshua possessed a "consumate knowledge of the Indian character," he was also a man "entirely too dark to be seen through." "There are but few who know him," the writer cautioned, "though they may have been long acquainted with him." He charged in particular, that Joshua's traders had deliberately fired upon the Rees at Fort Recovery in the spring of 1823 to provoke the Indians to block river commerce so that Ashley could not reinforce and supply Henry, who was competing with Jones and Immell on the Yellowstone. He also charged that Joshua had agreed to accompany the expedition north from Fort Recovery only after he heard of the disaster to Jones and Immell, and that his intention was to plunder the Ree villages of horses that he needed to send traders overland from the Sioux country to the "Big Horn River, and the Sources of the Arkansas" to replace the trade lost to the Blackfeet. The Sioux, he claimed, deserted the battlefield at an inopportune moment only because Joshua, Campbell, and Paul Dorion (a Sioux interpreter) worked at cross purposes.

The letter writer also castigated O'Fallon, McDonald, and Moses Carson. He maintained that "British Traders had [not] improperly interfered with our Indians"; asked "how long this Nation will continue to listen to falsehood & folly and to believe that those Trappers are deserving of the National protection"; and reported that Joshua had said he *"thirsted for the Blood of the Indians, as a new born babe for its mothers milk."* Perhaps the letter writer was misinformed, perhaps he was vindictive for reasons unknown—or he may have interpreted Joshua's motives accurately. At times Joshua *was* "entirely too dark to be seen through."[24]

[24] Anonymous to Thomas[?] Forsyth, January 23, 1824, Forsyth Papers, Draper Collection of Manuscripts (Microfilm of the Draper Collection in the State Historical Society of Wisconsin), Rice Institute, Houston, Texas. Doane Robinson (see footnote 19) reaches similar conclusions (pp. 235–36).

JOSHUA PILCHER AND COMPANY

T HE ARMY's first major Indian engagement on the upper Missouri fizzled out in the smoking embers of the Ree villages. The enemy disappeared; the Sioux sulked; the infantry returned ingloriously to Fort Atkinson; Ashley retired to Fort Kiowa to re-examine his trading plans; and Joshua retreated to Fort Recovery. No one was pleased with the outcome of the expedition. Everyone had lost something: Ashley, men, supplies, and time; Leavenworth, equipment and the respect of those of his infantrymen who wanted to beat the Rees resoundingly; Joshua, the loyalty of his Sioux allies, and, as usual, his temper. The campaign had been peculiar. The army, under Leavenworth, favored more moderate peace terms than the Indian agents: usually it was the other way round. The victors could not even agree on how many casualties the Rees had suffered: Joshua estimated thirty or less, but Leavenworth said fifty or more. And almost before the shooting war was over, the paper war between the soldiers and the civilians began, to continue until nearly everyone was worn out and disgusted with it all.

Joshua fired his first shots in the prolonged pen-and-ink skirmish within a few days after he returned to Fort Recovery from the Ree villages. First he complained to his friend O'Fallon of the failure of the campaign, and O'Fallon, in his correspondence, agreed with Joshua that the military were to blame. Then, on August 26, Joshua wrote a bitter letter to Leavenworth in answer, he said, to an order issued by Leavenworth eleven days earlier, on August 15, accusing the Missouri Fur Company of setting fire to the villages "contrary to the most positive orders, and in violation of their word of honor to obey orders."[1] Joshua took pride in his "desire to establish candure as the most prominent feture [*sic*] in [his] character" and, viewing Leavenworth's order as a "wanton attack," answered it in kind.[2] He charged that the attack on the villages was disorganized throughout; that Leavenworth's hatred of him—he dated it from the peace parley on August 10—prejudiced the Colonel's thoughts and action. He liberally sprinkled the letter with venom, picturing Leavenworth as a man of a "thousand tongues . . . [with a] face for every tongue," swayed by "little contemptible jealousies," who retired to his boat to sleep or pretend to sleep "in the hour of battle and of danger" and hid behind the "mighty shields" of "humanity and philanthrophy." The letter is a prize essay in abuse, but is it accurate? Unfortunately, the Ree campaign was not a game, there were no neutral referees on the battlefield, and we have only Joshua's word, supported by *his* friends, pitted against Leavenworth's word, supported by *his* friends. In such an engagement truth loses the field.[3]

Within a few weeks of the campaign the St. Louis newspapers acquired copies of Joshua's indictments of Leavenworth and printed them. Other newspapers reprinted the letters. Leavenworth's friends rose to defend him in additional letters to the editors; Joshua's friends answered in kind, and denunciations flew thick and fast. Perhaps if Joshua had heeded the words he had written earlier, he might not have set the whirlwind spinning from west to east. In 1817 he had written to Stephen F. Austin: "There are two classes of men in the world who in my opinion are equally contemptible," the friend who cannot be trusted and "the officious news gatherer who goes about collecting trash."[4]

[1] Leavenworth's Order of August 15, 1823, reprinted in Donald McKay Frost, *General Ashley The Overland Trail And South Pass*, 99.

[2] Joshua Pilcher to Ramsay Crooks, June 16, 1822, Chouteau MSS, MoSHi.

[3] Joshua Pilcher to Colonel Henry Leavenworth, August 26, 1823, reprinted in Frost, *Ashley*, 98–108.

[4] Joshua Pilcher to Stephen F. Austin, May 14, 1817, reprinted in Barker (ed.), *Austin Papers*, II, 307.

The trash piled up during the winter of 1823–24. The *St. Louis Enquirer* and its competitor, the *Missouri Republican*, both eager to increase circulation, responded to the "eagerness manifested by the public" for news on the Ree controversy by printing every available document.[5] The *Missouri Intelligencer* at Franklin—the town was an important river port in the fur trade—took particular interest in the argument. The editor of the paper, however, refused at first to publish Joshua's charges although he held Joshua in the "highest respect" and believed him to be "a man of unquestioned and unquestionable veracity." It was evident, he wrote, that Joshua's letters were "written under a high state of excitement" and added, "Honorable minds are always ardent, and in the warmth of his feelings, Mr. Pilcher may have been betrayed into a severity and harshness of expression which he would not, in the moments of coolness, resort to." The editor sought to remain neutral in the battle, but the partisans of both Joshua and Leavenworth took up their ink-stained cudgels and waded into the fight. "Cowpens," a "soldier of the old school," denounced Joshua for attacking Leavenworth. Immediately, "A Mechanic" defended "honorable and high-minded . . . industrious, persevering, faithful" Joshua. He praised Joshua's writing style, dignity, "pure soul . . . elevated mind, perseverance in business, ardor and generosity in his friendships"—but admitted he had never met him![6]

The army defended Leavenworth publicly and privately and praised Ashley for his co-operation in the Ree campaign. General Gaines reflected the view of the entire Western Department of the army in a letter to Secretary of War John Calhoun on October 16. Leavenworth, Gaines stressed, "had a right to decide as to the

[5] *Missouri Republican* (St. Louis), October 8, 15, November 5, 26, 1823; *St. Louis Enquirer*, October 18, 1823.

[6] *Missouri Intelligencer* (Franklin), November 11, 18, 25, December 16, 1823.

hree Siouan Indians: *left to right*, Missouri, Oto, and Ponca. From a painting
by Charles Bodmer in Maximilian's *Travels*.

Arikara Indian,
from a painting by
Charles Bodmer in
Maximilian's *Travels*.

measure of punishment due to the enemy, and to dictate to him the terms of capitulation," and sounded a high moral note that few civilized men could contradict: "The victory most acceptable to an enlightened and virtuous nation is, doubtless, that which is obtained at the least expense of blood."[7] The hubbub in the newspapers continued into 1824, and there was some speculation about a possible Congressional investigation of the entire Ree question. In the House of Representatives Charles Rich of Vermont read Joshua's and William Gordon's letters on the Jones and Immell massacre and introduced a resolution instructing the Committee on Indian Affairs "to inquire into . . . measures" to restrain white men from hunting and trapping on Indian lands. The resolution carried, but the Congress launched no full-scale examination of the Ree affair.[8]

The Senate Committee on Indian Affairs also examined the Indian trade and, through Benton's good offices, sent Joshua a list of questions on the problem. Joshua answered the questions fully in a long letter to the committee dated March 18, 1824. In remarkably moderate language he reviewed the events leading to the Ree war, discussed the characteristics of the upper Missouri tribes, and reflected upon the future of the United States in the Northwest. He emphasized the danger of British traders to American control of the Missouri River fur trade and urged that the federal government place a "small garrison [at Council Bluffs], one at or near the Big Bend, one at the Mandans, and the principal one at or beyond the Yellow Stone." Then, at the end of the letter, he added "a few [unsolicited] observations relative to the system": he criticized Ashley's practice, although he did not mention Ashley by name, of sending white trappers into the In-

[7] General Edwin P. Gaines to Secretary of War John Calhoun, October 16, 1823, *American State Papers*, II (Military Affairs), 596.

[8] *The Debates and Proceedings in the Congress of the United States* (December 1, 1823–May 27, 1824), cols. 896–97.

dian country, and recommended that white men be restricted to trading posts in locations selected by Indian agents; that the agents investigate the posts frequently; that white traders be prohibited from wandering, without good reason, from the posts into the Indian country; and that only licensed traders be allowed to reside in the Indian country. He reminded the committee that good-quality, reasonably priced trade goods "can be made in the United States" and, from his point of view, should be used in the fur trade in place of foreign imports.[9]

While newspaper editors argued over the Ree campaign and congressmen probed the Indian trade, Joshua picked up the pieces of the Missouri Fur Company that were left and kept trade going as best he could. He had ordered Fort Vanderburgh destroyed during the summer of 1823 when it became obvious that the post might be isolated by the Rees. The garrison, under Charles Keemle, had abandoned the site and descended the Missouri to join Joshua near the Ree villages shortly before the battle opened. Now there was no Missouri Fur Company post north or west of Fort Recovery, to which Joshua had returned after the Ree campaign, boiling with rage against Leavenworth and exerting every effort to retain the Sioux trade. Game was scarce along the river—the buffalo had fled when the Ree expedition moved upstream—and the Sioux looked to Joshua for supplies. If he failed them, he might never regain their trade.

Just when he needed time to think and to obtain supplies to humor the Sioux, a distinguished European traveler, Prince Paul Wilhelm, Duke of Wuerttemberg, and his entourage rode up to the fort. Joshua welcomed the Prince "in the friendliest manner" and invited him "to spend some time in that region." What else could he do? Joshua's friends and enemies downriver had extended the nobleman their hospitality; he could do not less at Fort Recovery. The Prince planned to continue upriver, "perhaps as

9 "Mr. Pilcher's Answers," March 18, 1824, 18 Cong., 1 sess., *SD No. 56.*

far as the Mandans," but Joshua dissuaded him: the Rees were dangerous, Fort Vanderburgh had been destroyed, and no princely escort was available. "Much to [his] displeasure, Prince Paul contented himself" with viewing the immediate environment for a few days. He visited the Sioux who were encamped on the prairie surrounding the fort, visited Fort Kiowa briefly on August 26, and took leave of Joshua, his "pleasant host," three days later. Joshua sent his clerk to escort the Prince and his baggage downriver in a small Missouri Fur Company boat manned by a cosmopolitan crew consisting of "two Americans, an Irishman, two half-breeds and a negro."[10]

While Joshua cultivated the friendship of the Sioux at Fort Recovery, following Prince Paul's visit, he heard that Henry had set out for the Yellowstone and that Ashley, assisted by the French Fur Company at Fort Kiowa, was outfitting young Jedediah Smith to lead a trapping party overland to the Crow country. Joshua lacked the supplies and trade goods necessary to equip a new party for the Blackfoot trade and had few men to spare for a long upriver trip to the Yellowstone, but he could outfit a small group to follow Smith to the Crow villages in Wyoming. Keemle and Gordon, survivors of the Jones and Immell massacre, were willing to lead the party, so Joshua equipped them and pointed them west in the footsteps of Smith, who had left Fort Kiowa late in September. The parties met on the western edge of the Black Hills, shortly after Smith had been mauled by a grizzly bear, and traveled close together through the Powder River country to Wind River, where they wintered with the Crows.[11]

As soon as Keemle and Gordon were on their way west and the Sioux had been taken care of, McDonald resumed com-

---

[10] Paul Wilhelm, Duke of Wuerttemberg, "First Journey to North America in the Years 1822 to 1824," in William G. Bek (ed. and trans.), *South Dakota Historical Collections*, Vol. XIX (1938), 401–10.

[11] Morgan, *Smith*, 85–86.

mand of Fort Recovery, and Joshua dropped downriver to Council Bluffs. Since Fort Lisa belonged to the Lisa estate and was rather dilapidated, earlier in the year the company had built a new post, Bellevue, closer to the mouth of the Platte River, below present Omaha and old Fort Lisa. Joshua ordered affairs at Bellevue for the winter and then set out for St. Louis to discuss company business with Hempstead and defend his name against Leavenworth's guerrillas. In St. Louis he wrote another letter to Leavenworth challenging again the Colonel's views of the Ree campaign and enclosed a statement, by Moses Carson, supporting the company position.[12] Joshua's letter, however, was only fresh fuel for the fire of partisanship and solved nothing. He left St. Louis on the morning of December 15 (if he stuck to his schedule) and traveled east to Washington, where he told Benton, the War Department, and anyone else who would listen, about the Ree campaign.[13] On the way, either to or from the capital, he probably visited his family in Lexington, but if he tried to influence the view of the editor of Lexington's leading newspaper on the Ree campaign, he failed: it was at about this time that the *Kentucky Gazette* cautioned the public to beware of complaints from traders since such men "are often influenced by mercantile cupidity."[14]

Pilcher family tradition holds that Joshua, during his fur-trading career, was engaged to a girl in Lexington. According to the story, passed along from generation to generation by Joshua's cousins, Hiram Shaw, Joshua's nephew, was escorting the girl to St. Louis to meet Joshua when his wagon overturned while fording a stream or crossing a marsh. The young lady was drenched,

[12] Joshua Pilcher to Colonel Henry Leavenworth, December 14, 1823, reprinted in Frost, *Ashley*, 115–19.

[13] Benjamin O'Fallon to Joshua Pilcher, January 18, 1824, Benjamin O'Fallon LB, 1823–29, CtY-WA.

[14] *Kentucky Gazette* (Lexington), quoted in the *Missouri Republican* (St. Louis), January 26, 1824.

developed pneumonia, and died before she and Joshua could be married. If there is any truth to the story, Joshua may have become engaged to the girl during his visit to Lexington during the winter of 1823–24, or, at least, may have met her at that time. Certainly, he was not engaged to her before he left Lexington in 1811 because he was engaged subsequently to a girl in Nashville and nearly fought a duel over another in St. Louis in 1817. His nephew Hiram (born in 1809) was too young to escort his uncle's fiancée to St. Louis before the late 1820's, and Joshua was not in St. Louis between the fall of 1827 and summer of 1830. The tale is poignant, and if not apocryphal, may account for Joshua's failure to marry—at least with license or benefit of clergy.[15]

By April, 1824, he was settled once again at Council Bluffs in a new "handsome trading House" at Bellevue.[16] Although the Missouri Fur Company was nearly bankrupt, he was determined to keep the post at Bellevue going until the partnership expired in the fall.[17] Evidently he remained at Council Bluffs during most of the spring and summer and, occasionally, accepted dinner invitations at Fort Atkinson or visited the post to allow Leavenworth's subordinates to examine his trading credentials.[18] The Missouri Fur Company, however, had little to trade with and, by May, only Bellevue to trade from: to conserve what remained of the company, Joshua had ordered his traders to abandon Fort Recovery.

[15] Pilcher Family Genealogical Notes, Mrs. Margaret P. Vaughan, Alexandria, Virginia.

[16] Russell Reid and Clell G. Gannon (eds.), "Journal of the Atkinson-O'Fallon Expedition," *North Dakota Historical Quarterly*, Vol. IV (October, 1929), entry of October 8, 1825.

[17] Tax List (Real Estate), 1824, St. Louis City Hall Archival Library, St. Louis, Missouri. This tax list assesses one "Joshua Pilcer [*sic*]" for items which may have belonged to the Missouri Fur Company in St. Louis. Unfortunately, the key to the property assessed no longer exists, and we must guess what company equipment remained in Joshua's name in St. Louis.

[18] Wesley, "Diary of Kennerly," *Missouri Historical Society Collections*, Vol. VI (October, 1928), 64–69.

They had loaded their gear in two keelboats, probably burned part of the post, and floated downriver, landing at Bellevue in mid-May.

At Council Bluffs, Joshua's competitor B (Bernard) Pratte & Company, successor to Berthold, Chouteau and Pratte, was digging deeply into his trade, and Astor—he had finally forced his way onto the Missouri River—threatened even greater competition. Keemle and Gordon, in the Crow country, unknowingly held the life of the company in their hands, and in the spring of 1824 missed a golden opportunity that might have saved the Missouri Fur Company from bankruptcy. When Smith led his band of trappers out of the Wind River Valley, Keemle and Gordon stayed behind to trade with the Crows. The Crow ran off with their horses, and the traders were forced to return down the Big Horn, Yellowstone, and Missouri. Gordon reached Council Bluffs early in July with only a few pelts to show for his stay in the Crow country.[19] Smith, in contrast, had led his trappers into untouched beaver fields west of South Pass and handed Ashley a fur-trade windfall.

Joshua waited impatiently for the Missouri Fur Company partnership to expire late in September, 1824, and, meanwhile, marketed only the small amount of fur he had in St. Louis.[20] He was prepared to give up the fur trade temporarily—or perhaps even permanently—if he could find another challenging job. When he heard that his old friend O'Fallon and General Atkinson were being appointed federal commissioners to treat with the upper Missouri tribes, he asked O'Fallon, at least twice, for the job of secretary to the commission.[21] Although O'Fallon assured

[19] Benjamin O'Fallon to William Clark, July 9, 1824, reprinted in Morgan (ed.), *Ashley*, 82. See also an article from the *St. Louis Enquirer*, July 19, 1824, quoted in *ibid.*, 86.

[20] American Fur Company Ledger K, MoSHi.

[21] Benjamin O'Fallon to Joshua Pilcher, August 6, 1824, O'Fallon LB, CtY-WA.

him that his claim to the job was a good one, Joshua was not appointed to accompany the expedition when it ascended the Missouri the following year. There can be little question that he intended to use the job to help himself re-establish his upper Missouri trade, and it is perhaps for that reason that he was not given the position, although it is more likely that he was simply too controversial to fill a prominent position in any project dominated by the army, particularly in association with O'Fallon, who was still arguing with Leavenworth and even bickering with Atkinson over the Ree campaign.[22]

In the late summer or early fall of 1824, Joshua returned to St. Louis to close the books of the Missouri Fur Company. He had worked hard for five years to make the company solvent and successful, but he had failed. The company was bankrupt, its creditors were unpaid, and Joshua did not have enough cash on hand to open a business in St. Louis. There was little he could do but stay in the fur trade, build a new partnership, and try once again to make it profitable. Despite the bankruptcy he was able to negotiate for $3,175 worth of trade goods and to obtain a license on October 27, 1824 to trade with "different tribes within the Missouri Agency" for one year.[23] Then, while autumn weather held, he headed back to Bellevue with his new outfit and reopened trade with the Indians on a cash-only basis: his capital was short and he did not trust Indians to pay their bills. He put Fontenelle in charge of the supply room and the ledgers while he discreetly drummed up trade among the Indians, a new federal law preventing him from gathering furs directly from the Indians in their camps.

[22] Benjamin O'Fallon to Colonel Henry Leavenworth, July 25, 1824, and to the Officers of the Ree Campaign, July 17, 1824, *ibid.*; Benjamin O'Fallon to General Henry Atkinson, July 31, 1824, and Colonel Henry Leavenworth to Benjamin O'Fallon, July 27, 1824, LR, OIA, RG 75, NA.

[23] "Abstract of Licenses Granted to Persons to Trade in the Indian Country. During the Year Ending 1st September, 1824," 18 Cong., 2 sess., *HD No. 54*, p. 8.

John P. Cabanné of B. Pratte & Company, Joshua's neighbor and competitor at Council Bluffs, was a flexible businessman with an investment to protect. Because he knew Joshua was an adept trader and believed that his no-credit-to-the-Indians policy might disrupt trade in the region, he proposed a temporary trade agreement—for which Joshua may have been angling all along. Under its terms the Indians continued to draw credit at Council Bluffs and Joshua was guaranteed a quarter of the fur return. In exchange, he would supply a quarter of the trade goods and send a clerk to Cabanné's Post to oversee the trade, while Cabanné would send a clerk to Bellevue to work side by side with Fontenelle. Lisa would surely have hated to see his successor settle for such a small share of the Council Bluffs trade, but Joshua was happy to take what he could get.[24]

Although Joshua's agreement with Cabanné was advantageous and assured him at least a small profit for the season 1824–25, he watched closely for other business opportunities and thought he had found one in the Southwest. Mexico had become independent of Spain and Americans were permitted to trade in Santa Fe, Chihuahua, and other Mexican towns. In 1824 a single American wagon train—eighty-one men and twenty-five vehicles (anything that rolled)—traded goods of every description in Santa Fe and returned over the long dry dangerous trail to Missouri with a fortune in bullion and furs. Joshua did not have enough cash to outfit a wagon train, but he could scrape up enough money to take a wagon or two full of goods to Santa Fe or Chihuahua. He believed, and rightly so, that dozens of profitable business opportunities waited men of his caliber in the Southwest.

Some time in the fall or winter, he wrote to friends in Washington, D.C. requesting appointment as United States consul at Chihuahua. On March 5, 1825, President Adams nominated Joshua for the position, and the Senate consented to it two days

[24] Morgan (ed.), *Ashley*, 260 (n. 37).

later.[25] The immediate confirmation and the timing of the appointment suggest strongly that Joshua might have favored Adams in the extremely controversial election of 1824, although his friend Benton had supported Clay. Joshua may have disagreed with him over the presidential contest, but, evidently, Benton backed his old friend for the consular post, and hoping to encourage American trade in the Southwest, he shepherded a bill through the Senate and into law, early in 1825, appropriating $30,000 for an immediate survey of the Santa Fe Trail.[26] The prestigious federal appointment gave Joshua a stake—not permanent, perhaps, but possibly lucrative—in the Santa Fe–Chihuahua trade. In June he received his commission from Secretary of State Henry Clay, but his "private affairs . . . prevented [him] from leaving . . . immediately." Nevertheless, late in August he "determined to visit Chihuahua, spend the winter in that country, and return to St. Louis in the spring."[27]

Meanwhile, he watched his pennies and nurtured the fur trade at Council Bluffs through the warm spring days of 1825. By June, if not earlier, he had decided to build a new western trading empire to replace the promising one lost by the Missouri Fur Company two years before. This time he planned a realm that would reach from Chihuahua to the Rocky Mountains. He intended to devote part of his time and capital to the Southwest; part to the fur trade west and north of Bellevue. Fontenelle, Drips, Vanderburgh, and Charles Bent, loyal lieutenants from the Missouri Fur Company, agreed to become Joshua's partners in the fur trade. On July 4, 1825, the government licensed the five men to trade for one year at a dozen or more locations between "the mouth

[25] *Journal of The Executive Proceedings of the Senate of the United States of America*, III, 438, 443. See also the *Missouri Intelligencer* (Franklin), April 12, 1825.

[26] Chambers, *Benton*, 124–28.

[27] Joshua Pilcher to Henry Clay, August 18, 1826, LR, Secretary of State, RG 59, NA.

of Kansas River" and the mouth of the Yellowstone. They put up approximately $7,200 in capital, over twice Joshua's investment of 1824 at Bellevue, and launched the new bark-of-empire on rough seas.[28]

Valuable time had been lost, between 1823 and 1825, in the race to the unexploited Rocky Mountain fur fields. While he had ministered to the dying Missouri Fur Company and struggled to raise money for a new fur trade partnership, Ashley and Smith—Henry had withdrawn from the trade shortly after the Ree campaign—had explored the Green River country west of the Continental Divide. Their trappers had gathered pack after pack of prime fur and, at the annual summer rendezvous in the mountains, exchanged them for supplies sent from St. Louis. The rendezvous system worked well for Ashley, so well in fact that in 1826 he was able to sell out to three of his most reliable men before his gambler's luck could change. Five years later he won a seat in the House of Representatives.

Early in September, 1825, Joshua reached Bellevue, either directly from St. Louis, where he had received his consular credentials from the government and had formed his partnership with Fontenelle, Vanderburgh, Drips, and Bent, or from the Sioux country near Big Bend on the Missouri where he may have gone before returning to Council Bluffs. Jim Beckwith, the storytelling trapper who used the truth as it best suited him, said that Joshua and Ashley met briefly late in the summer. According to Beckwith, Ashley, descending the Missouri with approximately $50,000 in furs from the rendezvous, met Joshua at Fort Lookout and accepted a present from him—"a large grizzly bear for a plaything."[29] Beckwith's story may be false, and probably is, be-

[28] "An Abstract of Licenses Granted to Citizens of the United States to Trade with the Indians During the Year ending 1 September, 1825," 19 Cong., 1 sess., *HD No. 118*, p. 40.

[29] T. D. Bonner, *The Life and Adventures of James P. Beckwourth* (ed. by Bernard De Voto), 54–55.

cause Joshua reached Bellevue before Ashley passed the Bluffs and almost immediately was "attacked with violent disposition which confined [him] there" until April, 1826.[30]

Fortunately not completely bedridden, although restricted to Council Bluffs for the winter, he was able to make most of the important decisions for the partnership. On some days he felt well enough to hunt or to visit his old friend John Dougherty at Fort Atkinson. Dr. John Gale, the army surgeon at the post, and a fellow participant in the Ree campaign, probably treated Joshua during the winter.[31] Fontenelle, Vanderburgh, Drips, and Bent divided the work at Bellevue and in the field until Joshua recovered. By May he was up and about regularly, and the following month he traveled to St. Louis for the summer. This was his longest visit to the city in eight years; his first good opportunity to wander through the city on long warm days to see how much the community had changed in nearly a decade.

St. Louis, prosperous again, rode the tide of better times nationally and reaped local rewards from the fur trade, the overland trail to Santa Fe, and the burgeoning steamboat traffic. Santa Fe–bound traders bid against fur trade outfitters and "rather malicious and dishonest" French merchants, as one visitor labeled them, for supplies. Everywhere new two-story brick and stone buildings stood side by side with older garden-enclosed structures. Noise from "an abundance of coffee-shops, billiard-tables, and dancing rooms" filled the summer days with sounds that reminded Joshua of the more carefree days of his youth in Lexington and Nashville.[32]

[30] Joshua Pilcher to Henry Clay, August 18, 1826, LR, Secretary of State, RG 59, NA.

[31] Wesley, "Diary of Kennerly," *Missouri Historical Society Collections*, Vol. VI (October, 1928), 90–92.

[32] Charles Sealsfield, *The Americans as They Are*, 92–94; Bernhard, Duke of Saxe-Weimar Eisenach, *Travels Through North America, During the Years 1825 and 1826*, 97, 102.

His long illness and the clamor of the creditors of the Missouri Fur Company, forced him to re-examine his dream of a Chihuahua to the Yellowstone trading empire. To satisfy the creditors, and to keep his integrity, he "executed . . . individual notes to sundry persons for [his] proportion of the debts" accumulated by the company through 1824. In 1836, after "ten years hard service" to pay his creditors, he still was unable to meet the notes.[33] While in St. Louis, he took out a new trading license on August 15, 1826, authorizing Fontenelle, Bent, Vanderburgh, Drips, and himself (his name does not appear on the license, however; the clerk probably forgot to enter it) to trade for one year, with a capital of $7,058.07½, at nineteen places scattered from the lower Missouri Valley to the Big Horn.[34] Three days later, shortly before he left for Council Bluffs, he sent the State Department his resignation as consul to Chihuahua. "The peculiar situation of my pecuniary affairs," he explained, prevented him from leaving the United States "for the present."[35] His vision of trans-western trade was dead.

By mid-September he was back at Council Bluffs.[36] His four young partners divided up the field work for the winter while he settled in at Bellevue once again. Competition was fierce at the Bluffs and along the Missouri and its tributaries below the Mandan country. Try as he might, he failed to win a larger stake in the trade. If business conditions did not improve for the partnership by spring, he knew he might be forced to give up the fur trade altogether. The threat of future unemployment and his desire to remain in the Indian country and use his knowledge of

[33] Joshua Pilcher to Ramsay Crooks, No. 1415, March 24, 1836, American Fur Company Papers, NHi.

[34] "Abstract of Licenses Granted to Trade with the Indians," 19 Cong., 2 sess., HD No. 86.

[35] Joshua Pilcher to Henry Clay, August 18, 1826, LR, Secretary of State, RG 59, NA.

[36] James Kennerly Diary, 1826–38, Entry of September 13, 1826, MoSHi.

Indian affairs prompted him to apply for O'Fallon's job as Indian agent for the Missouri River tribes. During the three months between December 1, 1826, when O'Fallon resigned, and March 1, 1827, when the resignation took effect, "applicants . . . too numerous to mention" appealed to the federal government for the position.[37] Many of Joshua's friends wrote Washington in his behalf, but Dougherty, O'Fallon's sub-agent and interpreter, received the appointment in the spring.[38] Dougherty, in turn, late in May, recommended Joshua for the Prairie du Chien Agency: He is "a man of honor ability activity and experience . . . I do believe there is none of my acquaintance better, if as well, qualified . . . nor do I know a man who would be more apt to give General satisfaction."[39] Despite Dougherty's glowing prose, Joshua was not appointed.

By that time he and his partners were in desperate straits: he had lost his chance in Chihuahua—the Senate confirmed Charles W. Webber of Tennessee as consul on March 3—he had failed to win O'Fallon's job, and Joshua Pilcher and Company lost more and more of the fur trade each day to Astor's American Fur Company monopoly as it spread along the Missouri River.[40] Small traders were given little choice—either co-operate with the giant, retire from the trade, or get out of the Missouri Valley. For them cooperation with Astor was impossible; Joshua's pride would not allow it. With nothing to retire to, nearly broke, and liable for Missouri Fur Company debts, his only chance was to take the

[37] Benjamin O'Fallon to Captain William N. Wickliff, December 1, 1826, O'Fallon LB, CtY-WA.

[38] None of the letters written the Secretary of War in Joshua's behalf now exist. The only record of them appears in abbreviated entries contained in the Registers of Letters Received by the Secretary of War, particularly under dates of December 6 and 20, 1826.

[39] John Dougherty to T. L. McKenney, May 24, 1827, John Dougherty LB, 1826–29, MoHi.

[40] *Journal of the Senate*, III, 575–76.

third alternative: talk his partners into plunging into the mountain fur trade, in competition with Ashley's successors, in a last desperate gamble.

His partners agreed that it was time to abandon the Missouri River trade. The new Western Department of the American Fur Company harassed them everywhere, and the four young men probably were more than willing to substitute adventure in the mountains for hard work at the riverside trading posts. Why should a man wear himself out "procuring fire wood, building houses, sawing plank, building boats, farming [and] running from one post to another," as Joshua described the duties of a post-based fur trader, when he was losing money and might do better out in the field trapping beaver, living off the land, and seeing new country?[41] Would the mountain tribes be any more dangerous than some of the Missouri Valley Indians who still killed traders and robbed each other? Under the circumstances they thought it best for Joshua Pilcher and Company to assemble an outfit for the Rockies. So they bought whiskey at Liberty, Missouri, and possibly at several other towns; gathered men, trade goods, and horses; and planned an assault on the mountain fur fields beginning in the fall of 1827.[42]

[41] "Mr. Pilcher's answers to queries relating to the Fur Trade, & c," in "Message From the President," 22 Cong., 1 sess., *SD No. 90*, p. 47.

[42] J. P. Cabanné to P. Chouteau, Jr., September 8, 1827, Chouteau MSS, MoSHi.

66

A<small>T</small> <small>BELLEVUE</small>, during the summer of 1827, Joshua heard the latest news and rumors about the fur trade. Ashley was making money hand over fist in St. Louis marketing furs and outfitting the Rocky Mountain Fur Company led by Smith, David E. Jackson, and William L. Sublette. Smith and a small trapping party had spent the entire year 1826–27, between rendezvous, wandering over the Great Basin and California. Following the summer meeting of 1827 near Bear Lake, Smith took a second party to the West Coast, but this time he lost most of his men in Oregon and barely escaped from the Indians with his life. Other events important to Joshua and the fur trade were taking place at Council Bluffs. The army abandoned Fort Atkinson in 1827, moved downriver and broke ground for a new post, Fort Leavenworth (Joshua must have cringed when he learned the name), on the west bank of the Missouri, approximately twenty miles northwest of the mouth of the Kansas River. The strategic location gave the army a post where it could keep a watchful eye on the fur trade and the commerce to Santa Fe. At least one international event in the summer of 1827 influenced Joshua's future in the fur trade. Great Britain and the United States extended the treaty giving them joint occupation of Oregon and thereby postponed again the decision over political control of the Northwest. East of the Continental Divide Ashley's successors held the biggest chunk of the fur trade and fought doggedly to keep it; west of the divide the Hudson's Bay Company embraced the trade. Joshua hoped to slip into the mountain fur fields somewhere between the great antagonists without being crushed in the vise.

In September, 1827, at the tag end of summer, forty-five

mounted men leading pack horses laded with goods and equipment rode west from Council Bluffs toward the Platte River. Joshua and his partners had used the last of their capital to assemble the party. Together the men, the merchandise, and the 104 horses represented Joshua Pilcher and Company's main chance, the last chance, to survive in the fur trade. If they failed to win a foothold in the mountain trade by the rendezvous of 1828, they would be done for and might as well quit. They moved up the valley of the Platte—a route opened by Ashley and his men—to the forks of the river in western Nebraska. There, in the cool days of early autumn, they took the North Fork past Court House and Chimney rocks, the natural monuments on the trail. By the time they reached the upper Sweetwater west of the North Fork of the Platte they were afoot: Crow Indians had stolen their horses. Joshua must have sensed then that he would lose his gamble on the mountain trade.[1]

Winter was the immediate problem, so just east of South Pass he cached whatever "merchandise and property" his men could not carry and led them over the snow-covered Continental Divide down into the valley of the Green River. South Pass, he noted, was broad, gentle, and perfectly well suited to carriage travel. They encamped for the winter on the Green, or as Joshua preferred to call it, the Colorado River. For a short time luck was with them. They traded horses from the Snake Indians and, when the weather moderated in the spring, one of the partners recrossed the pass and dug up the cache, but, their luck had quickly disappeared. Seepage had destroyed a "considerable part of [the] merchandise" left in the ground, and the partners knew the game was lost.[2] Nevertheless, they moved west to Bear Lake for the

[1] Joshua Pilcher's Report to the Secretary of War, in "Message From the President of the United States, In answer to a resolution of the Senate relative to the British establishments on the Columbia, and the state of the fur trade, & c," January 24, 1831, 21 Cong., 2 sess., *SD No. 39*, pp. 7–8.

[2] *Ibid.*, p. 8.

Fort Armstrong, Rock Island.

Jasper House in winter. From Paul Kane,
Wanderings of an Artist (London, 1859).

summer rendezvous of 1828 and sold their remaining goods to the trappers, some of whom had barely survived the unusually severe winter in the mountains. Then three of the traders, Vanderburgh, Fontenelle, and Bent, hastened back to Council Bluffs from the rendezvous with "only 16 to 18 packs of beaver."[3] They asked Cabanné to outfit them for the mountains, but he refused.[4] Instead, he hired Vanderburgh to trade for him, with the Poncas in Nebraska, and he probably subsidized Fontenelle to help Drips run Joshua's old post at Bellevue. Dougherty wrote Vanderburgh a few months later that he was "always ready to do anything in [his] power for Pilcher, Drips, Fontenelle and yourself," but Dougherty was not a fur trade financier, only a good friend without much money.[5]

Joshua had stayed in the mountains rather than return to Council Bluffs defeated by the Indians, the weather, and his competitors. He gathered the remnants of his expedition into a small trapping party of eight trappers, his illiterate clerk Johnson Gardner, and himself, and at the end of the July rendezvous led them north on foot from Bear Lake. Game was scarce nearly everywhere. They picked their way slowly over the mountains, trapped a few beaver, and finally reached Clark's Fork in western Montana. Snow fell and drifts piled up, so they made winter camp in the timber near Flathead Lake on December 1, and waited for spring.[6]

In the quiet valley camp Joshua thought about his future. His trading company had died at the rendezvous, and his former

[3] J. P. Cabanné to P. Chouteau, Jr., September 22, 1828, Chouteau MSS, MoSHi.

[4] Ibid., October 14, 1828, ibid.

[5] John Dougherty to W. H. Vanderburgh, February 24, 1829, Dougherty LB, MoHi.

[6] Unless otherwise noted, the narrative of Pilcher's journey from Bear Lake, in 1828, to the Mandan villages, in 1830, is based upon his report to the Secretary of War cited in footnote 1 of this chapter.

partners had scattered. He was short of men, trade goods, and equipment. His small party had taken few pelts, and his prospects in the new year were poor. Nearly thirty-nine years old, in debt, and snowed in, in the heart of the Rockies, he needed to do something; needed to take some decisive step to rebuild his self-esteem and his career. As he thought of the future and considered his bad luck in the past, he hit upon an extraordinary idea, another empire-building plan. On December 30 he wrote a letter to George Simpson, governor of Rupert's Land (that portion of Canada ruled by the Hudson's Bay Company under the royal charter of 1670) at Fort Vancouver, offering his services to his old enemy the Hudson's Bay Company. Joshua proposed that the British supply him with goods in the spring, and send him east across the mountains to compete with American trappers and traders in the upper Missouri country. He offered to lead the Anglo-American expedition in his own name to get around regulations forbidding foreigners from trapping on American soil. Joshua was desperate, so desperate that he pushed aside integrity, national loyalty, and even common sense in a foolhardy effort to save his career.

Governor Simpson knew that Joshua was in trouble and that American trappers in the Northwest were at times impelled to seek goods and equipment from the British because there were no American supply stations in the area. Nonetheless, Joshua's offer was peculiar. Was it a trap? Probably not, but the Governor was unsure. He wrote Joshua on February 18, 1829, rejecting the offer on political grounds: "the territorial rights of the United States Government." Governor Simpson asserted that "although the protecting Laws of your Government might be successfully evaded by the plan you suggest still I do not think it would be reputable in the Honble Hudson's Bay Coy to make use of indirect means to acquire possession of a trade to which it has no just claim."[7] The

[7] Governor George Simpson to Joshua Pilcher, February 18, 1829, reprinted in Frederick Merk, *Fur Trade and Empire*, 307–308.

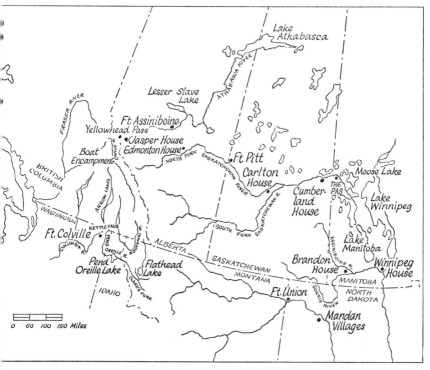

Pacific Northwest and Western Canada, 1828–30

Governor believed that the British fur brigades were capable of developing the northwestern fur trade without clandestine American help and may have enjoyed sending Joshua a "lesson in business ethics, for the bitterest critics of the Hudson's Bay Company in the American Government were the Missouri Senators Benton and [Lewis F.] Linn."[8]

[8] *Ibid.*, 308. This is Merk's comment.

During the winter Joshua visited the nearest Hudson's Bay establishment, tiny Flathead Post, and exchanged approximately half of the pelts, taken in the fall hunt, for supplies. He mounted his men on horses traded from the Indians or the British and, shortly after he received Governor Simpson's answer to his letter, late in February, headed north from Flathead Lake.[9] If he could make a good spring hunt and could hold his small trapping party together for a few months, he could go to the rendezvous of 1829 to bargain for the supplies and equipment he needed to stay in the fur trade. Late in the spring Indians stole his horses again and killed one of his men on the Kootenai River. His companions were thoroughly "disheartened with the sufferings and privations they endured," and Joshua admitted, in a grand understatement, that his prospects were not "sufficiently brilliant." Shortly after the Indian trouble on the Kootenai, he encountered a trapping party under David E. Jackson, partner of Smith and Sublette in the Rocky Mountain Fur Company. Joshua allowed his men to join Jackson's larger, better-equipped party; sold his traps to his competitor for $200; and, with one companion, backtracked to Flathead Post.[10] The worst had happened. He was Ishmael of the fur trade, a trapper without traps, a trader without trade goods. Fortunately, his health was good that year, and the Hudson's Bay representative at Flathead Post promised to lead him west to shelter on the Columbia River for the winter.

The trip from Flathead Post to Fort Colville was alternately easy and difficult. For the first five days they floated down Clark's Fork, across Lake Pend Oreille, and down the Pend Oreille River in a batteau, a shallow-draught flat-bottom boat tapered at each

---

[9] Dispatch from George Simpson to the Governor and Committee of the Hudson's Bay Company, March 1, 1829, reprinted in E. E. Rich (ed.), *Part of Dispatch From George Simpson Esqr Governor of Rupert's Land to the Governor and Committee of the Hudson's Bay Company London March 1, 1829. Continued and Completed March 24 and June 5, 1829,* 56.

[10] Morgan, *Smith,* 300.

end. Then they crossed a long portage from the Pend Oreille to Fort Colville, just below Kettle Falls, on the Columbia. Joshua remained at the post the first three weeks in September, enjoying "most kind and hospitable" treatment from the two dozen men stationed there. Life in the log houses in the fort was reasonably comfortable; the daily menu included dairy products, bacon, homemade bread, and a great variety of vegetables raised on the sixty- to seventy-acre post farm. Joshua rested, filled up on excellent food, watched the men of the post build a stockade around the buildings, and decided not to follow his original plan to descend the Columbia River to the sea to find a ship bound for the East or Gulf Coast. He accepted, instead, company permission to accompany their express east across Canada. Since the express trip took less time than a sea voyage, he could be in St. Louis by spring.

On September 21, Joshua left Fort Colville with six company men carrying the annual winter express (letters and business documents) to York Factory, on Hudson Bay, and intermediate posts. They ascended the Columbia, from above Kettle Falls, in a four- or five-ton batteau, through the Arrow Lakes and past the foot of Mount Revelstoke to Boat Encampment at the Great Bend in the Columbia where the river sweeps southeast between the Continental Divide and the Selkirk Mountains. The scenic three-hundred-mile upriver trip to the bend took two weeks. They landed at Boat Encampment on October 4, nearly a month before the express from Hudson Bay rode in on November 2. From the eastern express Joshua learned the latest year-old news. Jackson had been elected President. That meant that Benton—the Senator had switched from Clay's to Jackson's political camp before Joshua left Council Bluffs—was in position to help his old friend secure a federal job if he wanted one.

The eastern express (westbound) gave its horses to the western express (eastbound) and took the batteau down the Columbia. Joshua and the western express left Boat Encampment on Novem-

73

ber 4 and followed a trail north along Canoe River. Three days later they ascended the main ridge of the Rockies to Yellowhead Pass. Atop the Continental Divide they left behind the mild weather, ice-free streams, and heavily timbered, grassy valleys of the western slope and plunged with "great difficulty" through heavy snow into the icy blast of mid-winter in a "wild, desolate and dreary" landscape covered with stunted timber. Below the main ridge, approximately 150 miles from Boat Encampment, they found shelter for nearly two weeks at little Jasper House, an isolated Hudson's Bay Company post maintained principally to accommodate travelers crossing the mountains between the Columbia and Athabasca rivers.

Joshua and his five hungry companions—one had returned to Fort Colville from Boat Encampment—greatly strained the Jasper House food supply. The post trader noted in his journal on November 11, the day the party arrived: "God knows for not bien told of thos arrivels we will all starve."[11] Phonetic spelling notwithstanding, the trader made his point and put his guests on half-rations while his Indian hunters foraged for meat. But game was scarce, the post all but run out of meat within five days, and the visitors had to live on one deer for a week, until a hunter killed two sheep. Meanwhile, snow or rain fell almost every day, and the wind blew, blew, blew. When the weather moderated on November 26, Joshua and the expressmen, guided by an Indian from Jasper House, set out overland across the foothills, southeast to Edmonton House on the North Fork of the Saskatchewan.[12]

For seven days they struggled through deep snow and fallen timber towards the plain; then gave up the battle and retreated to

[11] Jasper House Post Journal, 1829–30, entry of November 11, 1829, B.94/a/2, HBCo (Film IM 65), PAC. This material and all subsequent material cited in the footnotes, drawn from the Archives of the Hudson's Bay Company, is published by permission of the Governor and Committee of the Hudson's Bay Company.

[12] *Ibid.*, entries of November 12–26, 1829.

Jasper House. By December 2 they were again at the post and, as before, food was short. "God knows how I mos go about with so many people to feed," the trader confessed in his journal, "and the hunter not able to Kill." To help keep everyone alive, the trader sent the expressmen to live and catch fish at a nearby lake. When the hunters killed mountain sheep and brought in a supply of meat he put the Indian women to work pounding some of it into pemmican. During the wait for better weather he made long (four- to five-foot) wicker snowshoes, pointed at each end, and built wooden sleds, with Joshua's help. In mid-December he sent for the men at the lake. Unfortunately, fishing had been poor and the men returned to the post hungry. Two of them were unable to travel and remained at the fort while the trader, Joshua, and six others loaded their packs with 120 pounds of pemmican and, on December 17, set out on snowshoes for Fort Assiniboine, the roundabout way to Edmonton House.

On New Year's Day, 1830, they reached their destination, a small way station and trading post on the Athabasca River some 150 miles northeast of Jasper House. They walked on the river ice most of the way through "very bad weather and two feet of snow." The "old man" from Jasper House, as Joshua called him, led the way, followed by the seven other half-frozen travelers and a sled-load of Joshua's baggage pulled by two dogs. Although they lived on the meager rations of a pound of dried meat each day for each man, they ran out of food late in December and went hungry for two days before reaching Fort Assiniboine. Joshua relaxed at the post for three days, and then left for Edmonton House accompanied by a traveler from the north. The trader from Jasper House gathered his spring supplies together at Fort Assiniboine and was back at his post in mid-February.[13]

Joshua easily crossed the one hundred miles between the Athabasca and North Saskatchewan rivers in six days. By January

[13] *Ibid.*, entries of December 2–17, 1829, and February 18, 1830.

10 he was settled comfortably within the strongly stockaded, heavily bastioned walls of Edmonton House (Fort de Prairie). The chief trader was friendly, and Joshua found ample provisions at the supply room to refill his packs. He bought a new gun, ammunition, clothing, and camping equipment, as well as Indian trading goods.[14] He stayed at Edmonton House five days observing how the company conducted the Blackfoot trade and then, on January 15, started down the North Saskatchewan with two expressmen. He planned to head south from Fort Carlton, east of Edmonton House, trading his way from tribe to tribe southeast across Canada into the upper Missouri Valley and on to Council Bluffs and St. Louis.

Between January 15 and February 1 Joshua and the expressmen traveled downriver approximately 450 miles. They averaged twenty-five miles a day on snowshoes over the surface of the ice-covered river and cross-country at river bends. Joshua walked through the snow most of the way, but rode occasionally, pulled by three dogs, in the baggage carriole (sled), built by the chief trader at Edmonton House for the convenience of his American guest. They stopped one day at Fort Pitt, a new Indian trading post located a few miles east of the present Alberta-Saskatchewan border, then pushed on quickly to old Carlton House, an "extensive" post, as Joshua remarked, located between the forks of the Saskatchewan.

The chief trader welcomed them to the post about nine o'clock on a "clear fine" morning, February 1, and made Joshua comfortable in the post. The following night the weather turned "very boisterous . . . with a Fall of Snow which continued the greater part of the forenoon." Joshua asked for a guide to lead him south to the Missouri River, but all the post employees were busy hunting, cutting firewood, making nails, or carpentering, and so he

[14] Edmonton Account Book, 1829–30, Account of J. Pilcher, January, 1830, B.60/d/33, HBCo (Film IM 469), PAC.

decided to go east with the York Factory express. On February 11 the Athabasca express arrived late, delayed by heavy snow. The following "calm, clear, mild" morning, February 12, Joshua finally departed for Cumberland House, the next post on the trail east.[15]

Now the journey was more difficult. The prairie ended a short distance from Carlton House, and the heavily timbered parkland closed in around the travelers. They followed the Saskatchewan, and cut across bends in the stream. Although the dogs had trouble pulling the carriole through the deep snow and fallen timber, the two young expressmen, "vigilant, active, [and] faithful" company-trained Indians, "full of resources" to cope with the hazards along the trail, brought Joshua and his dog sled safely through nearly 250 miles of wilderness in thirteen days. Joshua stayed at Cumberland House two nights, February 24–26; bought an axe, tobacco, gunpowder, balls, and shot, and on the morning of the twenty-sixth continued downriver with the Swan River express through the Pas of the Saskatchewan into west-central Manitoba.[16]

He passed a small trading post at Moose Lake on March 1 and separated from the express a little later. Apparently with the help of an Indian guide, he proceeded southeast on the river across the ice from lake to lake to Winnipeg Post (Fort Garry) where Donald McKenzie, governor of Assiniboia, welcomed him warmly to the Red River colony. For the first time in years Joshua saw the "cheering aspect" of orderly farms, comfortable homes, a school, and a church. He mingled with the cosmopolitan population, Scots, English, French, and Métis, until March 27. Then, just before midnight, when the snow and ice had frozen hard enough

[15] Carlton House (Saskatchewan) Post Journal, 1829–30, entries of February 1–12, 1830, B.27/a/18, HBCo (Film IM 19), PAC.

[16] Cumberland House Account Book, 1829–30, Enclosure Account of Joshua Pilcher, February 25, 1830, B.49/d/27, and Cumberland House Post Journal, 1829–30, entries of February 24–26, 1830, B.49/a/45, HBCo (Film IM 460 and 41), PAC.

to walk on, he started west up the Assiniboine River with a Métis guide hired at Red River.[17] Owing to the softness of the snow during the day they could only travel from midnight to 10:00 A.M., and, consequently, did not reach Brandon House until April 3. Although the chief trader admitted in the post journal that he did not expect visitors, he was cordial to Joshua and "advanced him goods to the amount of seven pound Sterling & supplied him with the requisite necessities for his Journey." Late in the evening the following day, April 4, Joshua headed south toward the international boundary line and the Mandan villages. "As he was only accompanied by one man," the Métis guide, the trader at Brandon House sent a post servant and a carriole and dog "with him for a days march."[18]

Hampered by the spring thaw, the trip south from Brandon House to the Souris (Mouse) River, up the Souris into central North Dakota, and across country to the Missouri River took eighteen days. On April 22 he reached the Mandan villages and met many friends, including the old fur trader Daniel Lamont, now of the American Fur Company; fellow Virginian John F. A. Sanford, sub-agent to the Mandans; his former aide Colin Campbell; and Prince Paul Wilhelm, Duke of Wuerttemberg, on his second trip to the upper Missouri.[19] A few days later Joshua and Sanford accompanied Lamont and Campbell down the Missouri with a shipment of buffalo robes. They reached Fort Tecumseh, a new trading post near the mouth of the Teton River, on May 6,

[17] Winnipeg Post Journal, 1829–30, entries of March 24–27, 1830, B.235/a/ 13, HBCo (Film IM 153), PAC. In his report to the Secretary of War, written after Joshua returned to St. Louis, he said that he left Winnipeg Post late on March 29. The post journal, however, states that he departed late on March 27.

[18] Brandon House Post Journal, 1829–30, entries of April 3–5, 1830, B.22/a/23, HBCo (Film IM 17), PAC. Joshua reported to the Secretary of War that he left Brandon House April 5. The post journal states that he left a day earlier, April 4.

[19] Paul Wilhelm, "First Journey," in Bek, *South Dakota Historical Collections*, Vol. XIX (1938), 472.

and in the evening, two days later, Joshua, Sanford, and one other man continued downriver in a skiff.[20] In June, Joshua landed in St. Louis, completing his "extraordinary, if not incredible" round trip of two years and nine months from Council Bluffs to the Rockies, Rupert's Land, and St. Louis.[21]

St. Louis was larger, busier, noisier, and more congested than Joshua remembered. One foreign visitor, looking across the Mississippi from the Illinois shore, wrote that the city presented "a very gay appearance" in 1830. Its tin-roofed buildings glistened in the morning light, and the inhabitants, he remarked, resembled Europeans in their manners more than any other Americans he had met in the West.[22] On the other hand, hundreds of chimneys poured coal smoke into the air above the town. The inns and hotels varied greatly in quality; some were "very comfortable" places; others were simply miserable.[23] Pressed for money, Joshua, probably, moved in with the Riddicks or other friends during his visit to St. Louis.

Although he was no longer either an active Mason or an affluent merchant-banker, he still knew many influential St. Louisans who were willing to help him re-enter business or find a job. In the fall of 1830 the Indian Office in Washington received a letter recommending him for an Indian agency appointment. Additional letters from his friends trickled into the Indian Office during 1832 and 1833. The recommendations indicated, of course, that Joshua was shopping for a federal job once again. At least three of his advocates were powerful politicians: Governor John Miller of

[20] Charles E. DeLand and Doane Robinson, "Fort Tecumseh and Fort Pierre Journal and Letter Books," *South Dakota Historical Collections*, Vol. IX (1918), 115–17.

[21] Joshua Pilcher's Report, in "Message From the President," January 24, 1831, 21 Cong., 2 sess., *SD No. 39*, p. 8.

[22] S. A. Ferrall, *A Ramble of Six Thousand Miles Through the United States of America*, 122–23, 129.

[23] James Stuart, *Three Years in North America*, II, 342, 344.

Missouri, a strong Jackson Democrat; Henry S. Geyer, a promising lawyer and future United States senator; and Congressman Joseph Duncan of Illinois.[24] This was the sixth time that Joshua had held or was recommended for a place on the federal pay roll. Whether he realized it or not, he had found a new career. He was to become a professional officeholder—a spoilsman living off Jackson-Benton patronage.

Towards the end of the year 1830 he sent Secretary of War John H. Eaton a long, detailed report on his western journey.[25] Secretary Eaton forwarded the report to President Jackson, who presented it to the upper house in his message of January 24, 1831, in answer to a Senate request for information "relative to the British establishments on the Columbia, and the state of the fur trade."[26] Joshua's report, together with similar reports to the government from Ashley and Smith, Jackson, and Sublette, contained in the President's message, provided the Senate excellent up-to-date information on the West. Within a few months the reports were published in *Senate Document 39* of the second session, Twenty-first Congress. Those who read the Senate Document became aware of the complex geography of the West and of the extent of American penetration of the area. Although Ashley, Smith, Jackson, Sublette, and Joshua erred in some details, their general outline of western geography and history was sound and certainly the best available at that time. To some extent Joshua and the other fur traders were understandably prejudiced in favor

[24] None of the letters written the Secretary of War in Joshua's behalf now exists. The only record of them appears in abbreviated entries contained in the Registers of Letters Received by the Secretary of War (RG 107, NA), particularly under dates of October 12, 1830, January 31, 1831, January and December, 1832, and May 20, 1833.

[25] "Joshua Pilcher's Report" of December 1, 1831, in "Message From the President," 22 Cong., 1 sess., *SD No. 90*, p. 13.

[26] James A. Richardson (ed.), *A Compilation of the Messages and Papers of the Presidents 1789–1897*, II, 534.

of American rights in Oregon. They accepted our national destiny to expand across the continent and expected Americans to settle eventually throughout the area. If the information in the reports made settlement any easier, so much the better.

Congressmen who favored early American annexation of Oregon were particularly pleased with Joshua's report and used it "widely as an authority."[27] Although Joshua made only a few direct references in his narrative to British military strength in the Northwest—Fort Colville, he noted, was defended by "some swivels" and "common fire-arms," and Fort Vancouver, he believed, was becoming a British naval and military station "which was not expected to be yielded" to the United States when joint occupation ended in Oregon—he revealed his political thoughts in eight observations appended to the narrative. In observation one, entitled "As To The Command of The Fur Trade," he quoted from Alexander Mackenzie's journals on the exploration of western Canada, explained how the Hudson's Bay Company functioned in Rupert's Land and in the Indian country west of the Rockies, and emphasized the political advantages held by the company in North America. Then, in observation two, "As To The Reciprocity of the Treaty of 1818," he called for termination of joint occupation and urged that the international boundary line be extended along the forty-ninth parallel to the sea.

In observations three through eight he gave his opinions on "The Present State of the Fur Trade," on the land and climate of the Northwest, and on the "Number and State of the Indians." He admitted, in his summary of fur trade history, that he "saw nothing" while in Rupert's Land "to justify the opinion that [the

[27] Archer B. Hulbert (ed.), "The First Wagon Train on the Road to Oregon," *The Frontier*, Vol. X (January, 1930), 151. Not every American was convinced that wagons could be taken west. At least one gentleman wrote the *New England Magazine* (February, 1832) asking whether the word of Ashley and Pilcher was superior to that of Lewis and Clark and others who found wagon transportation impracticable in the Rockies (see Hulbert, 149–50).

Hudson's Bay Company] excited the Indians to kill and rob our citizens." Thus, Lisa's successor, now more than ever a man of the world, had changed his mind. On the tariff he had also altered his stand a bit from that he had taken in his buy-American statement to the Senate committee in 1824. Now he called for abolition of the tariff on imported woolen goods to give American fur traders a better competitive position with the Hudson's Bay Company, and he favored a duty on furs imported into the United States because American exporters paid foreign duties on furs shipped abroad.

He described the Oregon country as a bastion behind the Rockies, a stronghold that the Hudson's Bay Company would be reluctant to give up, and predicted that the Monroe Doctrine might yet be tested in the area. On the other hand, he stressed that the Rockies were not impassable mountains, even for wheeled vehicles, and that American settlers would flow westward through the mountain passes. Although the land and climate of the West varied from region to region, the area held rich, well-watered valleys—he pointed to Clark's Fork and Flathead Lake as suitable for settlement—good grazing lands, and fisheries. He characterized the northwestern Indians as more honest than the "begging, drinking, and lying" red men east of the Rockies and added that the Indian horsemen of the Oregon country could be trained, presumably by the British, to be a "formidable . . . irregular cavalry." Few Americans of Joshua's time traveled in Rupert's Land and none, in 1830, knew more than he about the Hudson's Bay Company posts between Fort Colville and Red River.[28]

During the 1830's and 40's American writers, urging settlers to migrate to Oregon, cited Joshua's report many times and quoted from it freely. Hall J. Kelley, one of the leading activists in the Oregon crusade, mined Joshua's narrative and all others he could find for information about the Northwest. He appealed to Ameri-

[28] Joshua Pilcher's Report, in "Message From the President," January 24, 1831, 21 Cong., 2 sess., *SD No. 39*, pp. 9–10, 13–20.

cans to cross the Rockies and settle the Columbia Valley. The important *North American Review*, of January, 1840, mentioned favorably Joshua's report, and, a few years later, extracts from the document were used to support one of the early transcontinental railroad-building schemes aired in the House of Representatives.[29]

Although Joshua explained to the Secretary of War in his report that he had "abandoned the [fur] trade myself," in the months following his return from Rupert's Land his creditors still hounded him for Missouri Fur Company debts.[30] While in St. Louis he was especially vulnerable to their demands, but in the year and a half, between June, 1830, and late fall, 1831, he spent considerable time in the city negotiating an appointment to the Indian service, living frugally, and perhaps earning money from his old hatter's trade. Throughout that period he maintained close contact with his friends at Council Bluffs and visited Bellevue—to sell bits and pieces of property left from Joshua Pilcher and Company?—and he, probably, even stopped at Fort Leavenworth a time or two to see where Dougherty, as Joshua remarked jealously and sarcastically, had "managed to get permission to *locate* himself" as Indian agent for the upper Missouri River tribes.[31]

[29] Katharine Coman, *Economic Beginnings of the Far West*, 116; *North American Review*, Vol. CVI (January, 1840), 118–20; "Railroad to the Pacific Ocean," July 13, 1846, 29 Cong., 1 sess., *HR No. 773*, pp. 17–20.

[30] Joshua Pilcher's Report, in "Message From the President," January 24, 1831, 21 Cong., 2 sess., *SD No. 39*, p. 16.

[31] Joshua Pilcher to William Clark, Late Fall, 1832, or Spring, 1833, LR, OIA, RG 75, NA.

THE REPORTS on the West submitted to the Senate by President Jackson early in 1831 whetted Congressional appetites for information on trade in the Indian country. Both William Clark, superintendent of Indian affairs at St. Louis, and Secretary of War Lewis Cass urged Joshua to send more material to the government on the history and the prospects of the fur trade. Late in the fall he responded, somewhat belatedly, to the requests. Clark and Cass were too prestigious to be put off indefinitely; the Indian Office was in Cass's department and Joshua wished to curry favor with the Secretary of War. On November 19 he sent Cass brief preliminary answers to twelve questions on the current state of the fur trade. He listed the American Fur Company posts on the Missouri River, described the conduct of the trade, and slashed again at high tariff duties on fur trade goods imported into the United States. He also sounded a warning note that would be picked up by conservationists in the next generation: "Fur bearing animals [were] diminishing rapidly" in the Indian country. Finally, he estimated that Americans had invested over two million dollars in the fur trade since the end of the War of 1812 and appended to his answers a list of traders killed by western Indians since 1819. He judged, however, that his "exhibit," compiled hastily in "a few hours' reflection," fell "far short of the actual number killed during the time alluded to."[1] Clark reviewed Joshua's statistics and similar figures sent in by Dougherty and estimated from them that 150 men were killed and 84 injured, and

[1] Joshua Pilcher to William Clark, November 19, 1831, Clark MSS, Vol. 6, pp. 378–81, KHi; "Mr. Pilcher's answers to queries relating to the Fur Trade, & c," in "Message From the President," 22 Cong., 1 sess., SD No. 90, pp. 46–48.

that $149,374 in property was lost between 1815 and 1831 in the western fur trade and the "Inland Trade to Mexico."[2]

To elaborate upon his preliminary answers, Joshua drew up and forwarded to Washington an annotated list of trading posts and sites located within the St. Louis superintendency. He designated specifically and accurately which tribes traded where in each of the five agencies—Upper Missouri, St. Peter's, Osage, Prairie du Chien, and Sac and Fox—and in the Mandan Sub-Agency included in Clark's jurisdiction.[3] He also sent to Cass a detailed analysis on western trade, dated December 1, 1831. In the first part of the report he summarized the history of the Missouri River fur trade between 1803 and 1827, the year the American Fur Company had monopolized the business on the river, and carefully explained how fur trapping differed from fur trading and how mountain trapping expanded after 1822 under Ashley and Henry. Joshua did not condemn fur trade monopolies simply because they were big and powerful. Instead, he remarked, "I have sometimes thought that a monopoly of the trade . . . would result eventually in as much benefit [to the Indians] as could be derived from an opposition, *provided*," and here was the rub, "*it were possible for such a thing to exist without abuse*" to the tribes. Having stung the American Fur Company and having dropped the monopoly issue in the lap of Congress, he reiterated his earlier statement that the fur supply was diminishing—if true, another touchy problem for Congress to think about—and turned, in the

---

[2] "Statement Showing the number of persons Killed while Engaged in the Fur Trade . . . ," November 20, 1831, LR, OIA, RG 75, NA. Evidently, Joshua dated the list one day in advance of his letter to Clark. Clark's "Tabular Statement" appears in "Message From the President," 22 Cong., 1 sess., *SD No. 90*, pp. 79–86.

[3] "Statement of the Location of posts for trade with the several Indian tribes within the Superintendency of Indian Affairs at St. Louis," in "Message From the President," 22 Cong., 1 sess., *SD No. 90*, pp. 63–64; William Clark to Secretary of War Cass, November 28, 1831, Clark MSS, Vol. 4, p. 308, KHi.

second part of his report, to questions of southwestern trade and frontier defense.

He reminded the government that traders moved over the Santa Fe Trail in constant danger of Indian attack. Even the best guides and ablest mountain men were not safe on the route. Jedediah Smith, Ashley's former partner, had been killed by Indians on the trail in the summer of 1831, and Joshua predicted that sooner or later "a whole *caravan* will share the same fate, unless some steps are taken to protect them." He begged "leave to suggest" that the army establish a post, approximately halfway between western Missouri and the great bend in the Arkansas opposite Mexican territory, garrisoned by infantry *and* mounted troops (dragoons) to protect the trail and to preserve "tranquillity [*sic*] upon our frontier." He thought it impractical for the army to place military posts in the mountains to protect the fur trade because the quartermaster could not supply the garrisons, and if the troops should compete with the Indians for game, the tribes would kill every white man in the region. Joshua estimated that it would cost the army more to pacify the mountain Indians than the "whole fur trade [was] worth." He also opposed military posts on the upper Missouri River "since [he had] discovered that [the Indian trade in the area] is generally a pretty good protection to itself, when once fairly opened and prudently conducted" (but was that possible if the American Fur Company monopolized the river trade?). He suggested that the army avoid building posts on the upper river by sending military expeditions upriver whenever necessary to subdue the tribes.[4]

The Senate printed Joshua's long report of December, 1831, together with his preliminary answers to questions on the Indian trade and his list of trading posts and sites in the St. Louis superintendency. Once again readers found controversial food for

[4] "Joshua Pilcher's Report," of December 1, 1831, in "Message From the President," 22 Cong., 1 sess., *SD No. 90*, pp. 11–18.

thought in his communications to the government. At least one pamphlet, now "excessively rare," was printed and circulated almost immediately containing selections from his reports of 1831.[5] Certainly, by the end of the following year many politicians, army officers, fur traders, and businessmen, east and west, knew who Joshua Pilcher was and had read or heard about his views on western trade and politics. Since Joshua never wrote of offering his services to the Hudson's Bay Company in 1828, his patriotism was never questioned by those who read his reports. Whether his readers agreed or disagreed with his opinions, they looked upon him as a loyal spokesman for American interests in the West.

In mid-December, 1831, less than two weeks after Joshua had sent his long report to the government, John F. A. Sanford landed in St. Louis with two interpreters, Michel Gravil and Loupon Frenier, and four Indian chiefs from the upper Missouri. The Secretary of War had authorized Sanford to conduct a delegation of Indian leaders east to visit President Jackson and see the marvels of American civilization. The administration, influenced by the American Fur Company, hoped to win the respect and confidence of the chiefs and, thereby, as Astor anticipated, stimulate the Indian trade on the upper Missouri. Sanford had planned to escort more than four Indians to Washington, but by the time he reached St. Louis from Fort Union, at the junction of the Missouri and the Yellowstone, his delegation had dwindled to one Cree, one Assiniboine, one Plains Ojibwa, and one Yanktonai Sioux. Deciding that four Indians were better than none, he arranged to leave for the East by water before ice closed the rivers to steamboat travel. But the Indians were ill for a few days in St. Louis, the Mississippi iced over, and Sanford was forced to change his sched-

[5] Peter Decker (comp.), *A Descriptive Check List Together with Short Title Index Describing Almost 7500 Items of Western Americana . . . Formed by George W. Soliday*, Part III, item 188.

ule and to take the delegation by stage from Missouri to Washington, D.C.[6]

Apparently, Joshua planned to visit the East early in 1832 to lobby with the administration for a job in the federal Indian Service, particularly for an appointment as Upper Missouri Agent. Although Dougherty held this position, Joshua coveted the important job. He believed that Dougherty was an idle, useless, and unfit agent and hoped to talk the Indian Office into firing Dougherty and hiring him.[7] Joshua also sensed—correctly—that Dougherty was associating himself gradually with anti-administration people and charged that he was an Ashley henchman. Now that Ashley was a member of the House of Representatives and a critic of the administration, the charge carried weight with Benton's group. Joshua met Sanford in St. Louis and either offered to help escort the Indians east or was asked by Sanford to assist him part of the way with the delegation. For one reason or the other he accompanied, at the government's expense, the group by stage from St. Louis to Maysville, Kentucky. At Maysville Joshua must have left the party to visit his family in Lexington, while Sanford guided the Indians east via Wheeling and Frederickstown to Washington, Baltimore, Philadelphia, and New York City.[8]

Joshua reached the capital late in January or early in February and began to pressure the administration for Dougherty's job. Dougherty defended himself vigorously in letters to his superiors and convinced Cass that he was a competent agent.[9] Joshua failed to unseat him, packed his bags in disgust and returned to St. Louis

[6] John C. Ewers, "When The Light Shone in Washington," *Montana, the Magazine of Western History*, Vol. VI (October, 1956), 2–11.

[7] Joshua Pilcher to Elbert Herring, April 24, 1832, LR, OIA, RG 75, NA.

[8] *Maysville* (Kentucky) *Eagle*, January 26, 1832; *Daily National Intelligencer* (Washington, D.C.), January 17, 1832.

[9] John Dougherty to Lewis Cass, March 1, 1832, LR, OIA, RG 75, NA; William Clark to Lewis Cass, May 15(?), 1832, Clark MSS, Vol. 4, p. 364, KHi.

late in March or early in April. Meanwhile, the House of Representatives debated Sanford's expense account for conducting the Indians to and from the east. Ashley, in "his *first effort on the floor*," as Joshua called it, objected to Sanford's request for $6,450 to pay the cost of the trip. "Never did a speech covering only one square in a news paper, contain so many errors," Joshua wrote to the Commissioner of Indian Affairs—but the sum was unusually large, and the administration was economy-minded.[10] Fortunately for Joshua's reputation, his share in Sanford's account was small ($201). Returning to St. Louis without Dougherty's job, he carried back, as a favor to the Indian Office, a package of Jackson medals for Clark and Sanford to distribute to the western tribes. He had made a good impression and built for the future in the capital. Benton still was on his side, and Representative John Bell of Tennessee, Chairman of the House Indian Affairs Committee, had asked him for his views on the Sanford controversy.[11]

Late in the spring an unexpected event pushed Joshua into the Indian Service faster than he had expected, in country unfamiliar to him. On May 27, George W. Davenport, the American Fur Company trader at Rock Island, Illinois, wrote Clark that Felix St. Vrain, agent to the Sac and Fox Indians, and three other men had been killed by Indians between Dixon's Ferry and Galena. Clark immediately called in Joshua and, on May 29, "temporarily appointed" him agent to the Sac and Foxes and ordered him "to proceed with all possible dispatch to the . . . Agency [at Rock Island], to take possession of the public property, with directions to visit different villages of the friendly Sac & Foxes & learn their movements." (Clark assumed that Sac and Fox Indians killed St.

[10] Joshua Pilcher to Elbert Herring, April 24, 1832, LR, OIA, RG 75, NA; Morgan (ed.), *Ashley*, 321 (n. 496).

[11] Sanford's Expenses for Conducting an Indian Delegation to Washington, 1832, Joshua Pilcher's Receipts of March 17, 20, 1832, and William Clark's Receipt of April 10, 1832, LR, OIA, RG 75, NA.

Vrain; he was wrong, Winnebagos had killed him.[12]) The appointment to Rock Island was not quite what Joshua had bargained for in Washington, but he dared not refuse it because he needed a job, and he thought that if he could run the Sac and Fox Agency efficiently, the government would be impressed and Dougherty might be easier to unseat. With this in mind he hurried north and took over the agency in the first week of June.[13]

Clark assured Cass that Joshua would "ascertain the real disposition & wishes of [the Sac and Foxes], and . . . devise and report in time, the best plan for their security," but that was a bigger problem than Clark imagined.[14] The Sac and Foxes had divided into several bands, some friendly, some hostile, and had scattered along the west side of the Mississippi River, from above the mouth of the Wisconsin to the Missouri line when the Illinois militia had forced them into exile the year before. In April, Black Hawk had led a large band of Sac and Fox men, women, and children back across the Mississippi River from eastern Iowa, to reoccupy their old villages and fields in the lower Rock River Valley. Immediately a volunteer force led by General Atkinson had barked at their heels; had driven them up Rock River to near Dixon's Ferry; and had fired upon them when Black Hawk had tried to make peace. The Indians had fled farther north, to hide in the swamplands surrounding Lake Koshkonong, and had sent warriors to raid the Illinois-Wisconsin frontier: if the whites would not allow his starving people to return peacefully to their fertile lands on Rock River, Black Hawk would give them war. By mid-summer scores of Indians and whites had been killed, and an army of volunteers moved through southern Wisconsin pursuing Black Hawk's band west towards the Mississippi River. But where was Black Hawk?

[12] George Davenport to William Clark, May 27, 1832, and William Clark to Lewis Cass, May 30, 1832, LR, OIA, RG 75, NA.

[13] George Davenport to Russell Farnham, June 8, 1832, Chouteau MSS, MoSHi.

[14] William Clark to Lewis Cass, June 8, 1832, LR, OIA, RG 75, NA.

This was the big question. He was rumored to be everywhere. Settlers in Iowa feared that the hostile Indians would cross the Mississippi, rejoin the peaceful bands of Sac and Foxes, talk them into war, and then attack along the frontier extending from northeastern Iowa to northern Missouri.[15] When Joshua stepped into the middle of the Black Hawk War, he had to find as many of the peaceful Sac and Foxes as possible, and he had to persuade them to remain neutral.

By the end of June, Joshua contacted the friendly Sac and Foxes on the Iowa shore west of Fort Armstrong and worked feverishly to keep them free of hostile influence. Two interpreters who were sent to accompany them on their summer hunt were to keep him informed if any hostiles reached the peaceful bands. He notified the Missouri militia, in position along the Des Moines River, that the Iowa Sac and Foxes he had seen were peaceful, and then visited the militia camp to verify that the force there was an authorized, rather than a vigilante, group.[16] It was authorized, and he promised Captain Richard Mace he would go to Fort Armstrong for the latest news on Black Hawk and return with the information quickly. Before Joshua could reach Fort Armstrong, he heard that Black Hawk had recrossed the Mississippi back into Iowa, and he advised the Missouri militiamen to ask for reinforcements.[17] The newspapers picked up the story and urged "prompt and energetic measures . . . [before] the very doors of our citizens are assailed by the savage foe."[18] To get additional details of the news about Black Hawk, Joshua dashed up to Galena, where he learned the story was inaccurate. Furious, he bewailed in a letter to Clark how rumor had undone nearly forty days' work.[19] If some trigger-happy Missouri militiaman

[15] William T. Hagan, *The Sac and Fox Indians*, Chaps. 12, 13, and 14.
[16] Joshua Pilcher to William Clark, June 28, 1832, LR, OIA, RG 75, NA.
[17] *Ibid.*, July 4, and 14, 1832, *ibid.*
[18] *Missouri Intelligencer* (Columbia), July 21, 1832.
[19] Joshua Pilcher to William Clark, July 14, 1832, LR, OIA, RG 75, NA.

had fired upon a peaceful Sac and Fox, the entire frontier west of the river might have erupted into war. The volunteer army found the trail in mid-July and finally caught and defeated the main band of hostiles at the mouth of the Bad Axe River early in August. Black Hawk, still trying to escape, was seized by a party of Winnebagos at the dells of the Wisconsin River and turned over to the white authorities. Few of the hostiles had crossed the Mississippi into Iowa, in the time of uncertainty, but Joshua did not know that until he received news of the battle on the Bad Axe and of Black Hawk's capture.

Despite the inflammatory rumors and the unwillingness of the Indian Office to feed all the peaceful Sac and Foxes until the end of the war, the Des Moines frontier remained reasonably calm. By mid-August, Joshua was settled again at the Rock Island Agency—the war was over. He helped Captain Patrick H. Galt interrogate the hostiles brought into Fort Armstrong and took a census, for the army, of all Indians, hostile and friendly, in military custody at the post. Joshua's greatest problem was Indian subsistence, and the regular appropriation for the agency was insufficient to provide it.[20] Could he stretch his limited supplies to support all the Sac and Foxes dependent upon his agency? Clearly, he could not. He could only be selective; distribute the supplies in his possession in accord with the "peculiar condition and circumstances" of each Indian.[21]

[20] Joshua Pilcher's Account, September 30, 1832, Clark MSS, Vol. 24, pp. 83–84, KHi; Abstract of Expenditures & Disbursements made by William Clark, October 1, 1831–September 30, 1832, 22 Cong., 2 sess., HED No. 137, pp. 51, 102–103; General Abstract of Disbursements or Expenditures by William Clark from October 1, 1832–September 30, 1833, in "Indians—Disbursements of Moneys, & c. For the Benefit of," 23 Cong., 1 sess., HED No. 490, p. 89.

[21] Joshua Pilcher to William Clark, August 23, 1832, LR, OIA, RG 75, NA. See also letters of September 3 and 8, 1832. The results of the interrogation of the Indians at Ft. Armstrong on August 18–19 may be found in the Andrew Jackson manuscripts at the Library of Congress. The Tennessee State Archives in Nashville holds copies on film.

Clark had appointed Marmaduke S. Davenport (no close relation to George W. Davenport) permanent Sac and Fox agent on July 10, but as Davenport could not take charge of the agency until November, Clark asked Joshua to remain at Rock Island until Davenport was installed properly. Joshua consented, although his salary, approximately $100 a month, was hardly adequate to compensate him for running the agency.[22]

On September 19, Major General Winfield Scott and Governor John Reynolds of Illinois, peace commissioners for the United States, opened negotiations with the Sac and Foxes at Fort Armstrong. By treaty, signed two days later, the Indians ceded to the United States as indemnity for the war and to secure the frontier against further Indian invasion, six million acres of land in a fifty-mile-wide strip bordering the west bank of the Mississippi River in Iowa. They promised to evacuate the area (the Black Hawk Purchase) by late spring, 1833, and the United States agreed to pay them $600,000 over a period of thirty years. The commissioners also agreed, as a humanitarian gesture, to provision the Indians for the coming winter, to deliver them six thousand bushels of Indian corn in April, 1833, to supply them with salt and tobacco for thirty years, and to build and furnish one additional "black and gun smith shop" for them in Iowa. Finally, "in full satisfaction of the claims of [Davenport and Farnham, the American Fur Company traders at Rock Island] against the said tribes . . . furnished in the course of the seven preceding years," the government promised to pay the traders $40,000.[23] Joshua was in St. Louis at the time the treaty was signed. He had suggested to General Scott that the General send him to St. Louis to obtain the $8,000 annuity due the Indians in 1832 and return it to Rock Island in time for the treaty-making. General Scott had

[22] William Clark to Lewis Cass, September 17, 1832, LR, OIA, RG 75, NA.
[23] Richard Peters (ed.), *The Public Statutes at Large of the United States of America*, VII, 374–76.

sent him downriver, but as he was delayed on the way and the treaty commissioners had proceeded with the treaty earlier than he had anticipated, he missed the negotiations.[24]

Although Joshua respected General Scott and Governor Reynolds as treaty commissioners, he believed they were unduly influenced by the traders, Davenport and Farnham, and vigorously denounced the treaty provision entitling the traders to $40,000 in claims payable from the federal treasury. He said that Davenport and Farnham had advanced the Sac and Foxes a small quantity of goods in the spring, shortly before the Black Hawk War broke out, anticipating payment from the annuity due the Indians, but when the treaty was being made, they had falsely claimed that the Sac and Foxes owed for goods supplied over several years; and when the treaty commissioners allowed the claim in his absence, they had permitted the traders to maneuver a few Sac and Fox chiefs into signing over the entire cash annuity that he was bringing from St. Louis. When Joshua landed at Rock Island, George Davenport demanded the annuity, but Joshua refused to hand over the money and put it, for safekeeping, in the magazine at Fort Armstrong. He then immediately wrote Clark a detailed explanation of the problem and impatiently awaited instructions from St. Louis, convinced that the traders intended to cheat both the government and the Indians, had lied to the treaty commissioners, and planned to use the new agent as a pawn.[25]

Joshua objected to the $40,000 stipulation in the treaty on three specific grounds. First of all, the provision had been written into the treaty without his (the Indian agent's) knowledge, an action that would destroy the confidence of the Indians in Indian agents and the government, and deprive those Sac and Foxes, whose chiefs had not signed the receipt given the traders, of annuity benefits. Secondly, he strongly objected to subjecting annuities to

[24] Joshua Pilcher to William Clark, October 16, 1832, LR, OIA, RG 75, NA.
[25] *Ibid.*

94

claims by private creditors because it was easier for an agent to supervise the Indians under his jurisdiction if he controlled their annuities. And, finally, his long experience in the fur trade had taught him that traders like Davenport and Farnham would falsify their records if necessary to defeat the Indian Office. George Davenport appealed to Pierre Chouteau, Jr., of the American Fur Company in St. Louis, to work on his friends in the Senate to guarantee passage of the treaty. He also suggested that if Chouteau could "alarm [Clark] smothley [sic]," about the safety of the money stored at Fort Armstrong, Clark would "probably order the money paid to us." Davenport was also irritated because he feared the enemies of the American Fur Company were "trying to get Marmaduke . . . out of office," and summed up his particular hatred for Joshua in a spurt of misspelled invective: "Their would be no dificulty if it was not for the interfeurance of Mr. Pilcher he is an evil genious equel to the Cholra if he had the same pour to scorge mankind, he has declared heur that he is determined to go to Washington to prevent our clam being passed by the Senate."[26]

Clark approved Joshua's position in the controversy—his principles were correct, he wrote Cass, and he acted in accord with government regulations—and the Indian Office agreed.[27] On November 13, when Marmaduke Davenport relieved him as Sac and Fox agent, Joshua reluctantly turned over to him the annuity on deposit at Fort Armstrong. Davenport gave him receipts specifying that the money was to be paid the Indians, according to government regulations, when they returned to the agency after the fall hunt. At the same time he assured Joshua that he knew nothing of the annuity problem, then, as soon as Joshua left Rock Island by steamboat for St. Louis on November 14, he turned

[26] George Davenport to Pierre Chouteau, Jr., October 12, 1832, Chouteau MSS, MoSHi.

[27] William Clark to Secretary of War Lewis Cass, October 22, 1832, and to Elbert Herring, November 27, 1832, LR, OIA, RG 75, NA.

$7,800 over to the traders. Later Joshua saw the money in six boxes aboard the steamboat *Winnebago* near Rock Island and immediately fired off a note to Clark telling him of the agent's perfidy.[28] Marmaduke Davenport, defending his action, said the Sac and Fox had asked him to give the money to Davenport and Farnham, but the Indian Office refused his wilted explanation and ordered him to distribute the annuity according to regulations. In April, Davenport and Farnham returned the annuity money to him. The Senate overlooked the attempt to grab the annuity of 1832, disregarded the fact that they had taken the annuity of 1831 by equally devious means, and accepted the Sac and Fox treaty containing the $40,000 provision.[29]

By the end of November, Joshua, still indignant over the annuity squabble, was in St. Louis for the winter. Anxious to help the Sac and Fox in some way, he recommended to Clark that the government move the Indian agency west—up the Des Moines River beyond the settlements, the liquor traffic, and the lawless men who roamed the Mississippi Valley. This was all he could do; his hands were tied. He could do nothing to rectify what the Davenports had done to the Indians, and he was too short of money to go to Washington to fight the treaty.[30] Fortunately for him, in November the Missouri Assembly re-elected Benton, his patron, to a third Senate term; Jackson carried the state by a two-to-one vote in the presidential contest, and the Democrats remained in power in Washington. During the winter Joshua renewed his campaign to force Dougherty out of the Upper Missouri Agency. Most agencies were built near army posts to afford

[28] Joshua Pilcher to William Clark, November 13 and 18, 1832, and M. S. Davenport to Lewis Cass, January 14, 1833, LR, OIA, RG 75, NA.

[29] Ruth A. Gallaher, "Indian Agents in Iowa," *The Iowa Journal of History and Politics*, Vol. XIV (July, 1916), 363–66; M. S. Davenport to Elbert Herring, April 12, 1833, LR, OIA, RG 75, NA.

[30] Joshua Pilcher to William Clark, November 26, 1832, LR, OIA, RG 75, NA.

the Indian agents military protection in carrying out their duties, and Dougherty had steadfastly refused Clark's requests to move the agency to Council Bluffs, away from the protection of Fort Leavenworth. In support of Clark's effort Joshua said that Dougherty could not properly operate an agency for the Missouri River tribes from any location south of Council Bluffs.

In a long letter to Clark, written in the spring of 1832, Joshua had charged Dougherty and his subordinates with neglecting the Indians in their care; operating the Missouri River Agency in the wrong place; wasting federal funds for five years; and failing to carry out adequately the provisions of the important Treaty of Prairie du Chien, of 1830, pertaining to the Missouri River tribes. He reviewed, year by year, the declining contact between Dougherty at Fort Leavenworth and the tribes at Council Bluffs and above on the river. If Dougherty lived at Council Bluffs, Joshua argued, he could prevent many of the incidents that now frequently occurred between the tribes in the valley and could properly carry out treaty provisions, particularly on annuities. Joshua estimated that Indian-white relations on the Missouri River were worsening and staked his reputation on that estimate because he was certain no one else knew the region and the Indians better than he.[31]

His declaration that he knew as much about the Missouri River tribes as anyone else, and probably more, was reasonably accurate. It was an honest statement that his friends accepted and his enemies contested. Above all, convinced that his words were correct, he repeated them frequently to politicians who controlled the traffic in Indian agencies. More and more concerned with the welfare of the tribes, he criticized federal Indian policy and urged that the Indians be treated fairly and justly. In his endeavor to understand how Indians viewed the white society about them, he examined Indian life carefully—so carefully that many of his letters and

---

[31] *Ibid.*, Spring, 1832 [?], *ibid.*

reports to the Indian Office, especially in the period 1835–41, deserve more recognition than they have received as documents valuable to the early study of Indian culture.

Joshua's new attack on Dougherty during the winter of 1832–33 failed. Dougherty remained in office at Fort Leavenworth, and Joshua searched desperately for employment. On March 26, Clark nominated him as a special or provisional Indian sub-agent to undertake the "arduous" task of delivering agricultural implements and merchandise to the tribes being settled in eastern Kansas under the Castor Hill Treaties of late 1832. Clark recommended that the Indian Office pay Joshua $500 a year salary (less than he had received at the Sac and Fox Agency) plus $700 in expenses.[32] Commissioner Herring approved the nomination as soon as he received it from Clark, but Joshua, "having been accustomed to an active life . . . could no longer brook the delay which was preying upon his health." On April 6 he accepted a better-paying job with his old adversary, the American Fur Company, with the understanding that he would give it up "should he be offered a permanent appointment in the Indian Department, for which he consider[ed] himself better qualified."[33]

Clark immediately employed William Gordon, Joshua's former lieutenant in the fur trade, to deliver the Indian goods and notified the Indian Office. At that point Joshua changed his mind again. Perhaps thinking that any federal appointment, no matter how temporary, menial, or difficult, would be better than a job with the Astor-Chouteau combine, he wrote Cass requesting the position that Clark had just given Gordon. Cass passed the letter to Commissioner Herring, and Herring told Clark to choose between Gordon and Joshua. Clark correctly took the position that Gordon had been appointed and that, although he knew of none "better qualified" for the job than Joshua, he could not remove

[32] William Clark to Elbert Herring, March 26, 1833, LR, OIA, RG 75, NA.
[33] Ibid., May 27, 1833, ibid.

Gordon.[34] Joshua had no choice now—either starve or carry out his contract with the American Fur Company. He swallowed his pride, resigned himself to work for the company for approximately two years, as they requested, and headed up the Missouri to his old trading-ground at Council Bluffs.[35]

[34] *Ibid.*; Elbert Herring to William Clark, June 17, 1833, and to Joshua Pilcher, June 17, 1833, LS, OIA, RG 75, NA.

[35] Joshua Pilcher to Pierre Chouteau, Jr., May, 1833, Chouteau MSS, MoSHi.

LATE ON THE MORNING OF APRIL 10 the American Fur Company's little side-wheel steamboat *Yellowstone* pulled away from the St. Louis levee bound for the fur posts along the upper Missouri. Most of the passengers, "about 100 persons," were company servants of the "lowest class," but a few distinguished travelers were also aboard, including German naturalist Alexander Philip Maximilian, Prince of Wied-Neuwied, and his companion, Charles Bodmer, a Swiss artist. The passenger list also included Dougherty, Sanford, Kenneth McKenzie, the company's ambitious trader from Fort Union, and Joshua, who had met the Prince in St. Louis and had favorably impressed him with advice about the Indian country. Joshua, under orders from Chouteau to take over, from Cabanné, the management of company trade at Council Bluffs, apparently, did not air his differences with Dougherty aboard the boat. Perhaps he had been advised by Chouteau not to harass Dougherty by tongue or pen while he was under contract to the company, or, more likely, he had decided, without Chouteau's advice, to allow the quarrel to cool off, because Dougherty had given in to Clark and was spending more time at Council Bluffs. Whatever the reason, they peacefully co-existed aboard the *Yellowstone* and got along reasonably well as neighbors at Council Bluffs for several years.

Early in May the boat landed at Bellevue, Joshua's old trading site, where Dougherty disembarked. By this time the post had expanded into a small community of white men "mostly married to women of the tribes of the Otos and Omahas." Over half a dozen families lived in huts on the riverbank or in the agency buildings on higher ground. Friendly, broad-faced Indian women, dressed in "red or blue cloth," worked in the fields bordering the settlement while their dark-haired, attractive half-blood children romped beside them. A few miles above Bellevue the boat stayed overnight, May 4–5, at Cabanné's Post, "a row of buildings of various sizes, stores, and . . . houses of the *engagés*, married to Indian women." Cabanné and Maximilian looked over the post and then, in the evening, they sat with Bodmer and Joshua on the balcony of the two-story main house enjoying the full moon hanging over the river. Noisy frogs and whippoorwills in the woods filled the night with sound until some of the Omahas gathered and danced for their illustrious visitors. After the dance the Prince and the painter took leave of Cabanné and Joshua and returned to the steamboat.[1]

The following morning, a "warm and serene" May 5, the *Yellowstone* headed upriver, and Cabanné started to take a final inventory at the post before turning over the business to Joshua. In fair condition, the buildings needed repairs, and the corn, in a small valley, above the stream that ran through the post, was not doing well. Joshua took charge of the buildings and crops, but he refused to assume responsibility for goods, belonging to a competitor, Narcisse Leclerc, piled in the powder house and the loft of the *engagés'* building, and wrote Chouteau promptly protesting "against the introduction of my name in connection with the aforesaid property, or the subject in dispute."[2] Cabanné had seized Leclerc's goods in the fall of 1832—the term "citizen's arrest" might best describe his high-handed procedure—and accused him of carrying liquor up the Missouri in violation of the new, July, 1832, Congressional prohibition on transportation of liquor into the Indian country. Leclerc had taken the company to court, and

---

[1] Maximilian, Prince of Wied, *Travels in the Interior of North America*, in Thwaites' *Early Western Travels, 1748–1846*, XXII, 236–75, and XXIII, 223. All the quotations in paragraphs 1 and 2 are from Maximilian.

[2] Joshua Pilcher to Pierre Chouteau, Jr., May, 1833, Chouteau MSS, MoSHi.

Cabanné had been called to St. Louis by Chouteau to participate
in the case. When Cabanné turned over the business at Council
Bluffs to Joshua and departed for St. Louis to testify against him,
Leclerc backed down and settled the dispute out of court, but the
controversy damaged Cabanné's reputation; from then on competing traders said the settlement indicated that the American
Fur Company would use any means to control the river trade.[3]

Joshua rearranged the pattern of life at the post to suit himself.[4]
He ordered his *engagés* to repair the buildings, to replant the
corn—Cabanné had either planted it improperly or the weather
had hurt the first crop—and to clean up the grounds. He bought
brooms, linseed oil and whiting for putty, paper, pencils, and
blank account books at Bellevue; requisitioned shingling nails
from St. Louis; and by mid-June reported to Chouteau that he
had put the post in "verry [*sic*] neat order."[5] The following
spring Maximilian, on his way downriver from his long visit to the
Indian country, stopped at the post and remarked that "there was
more order and cleanliness . . . than during our former visit."
Joshua had converted the second floor of the main building into a
storeroom—Maximilian estimated that in addition to buffalo and
beaver skins approximately 24,000 muskrat skins were "very
regularly piled up" in the large room—and had refurbished the
ground floor for his own living quarters.[6]

Joshua stressed cleanliness and orderliness at the post, carefully
watched the morale of his men, and saw to it that their squaws and
half-blood children obeyed his orders. Fifteen years' experience

[3] Hiram M. Chittenden, *The American Fur Trade of the Far West*, I, 346–50;
Phillips, *Fur Trade*, II, 423–24.

[4] Maximilian, *Travels*, XXIV, 106 (n. 84).

[5] Joshua Pilcher to John B. Sarpy, June, 1833, and to John P. Cabanné,
June 16, 1833, and to Pierre Chouteau, Jr., June 16, 1833, Chouteau MSS,
MoSHi.

[6] Maximilian, *Travels*, XXIV, 106; Joshua Pilcher to John P. Cabanné,
June 16, 1833, Chouteau MSS, MoSHi.

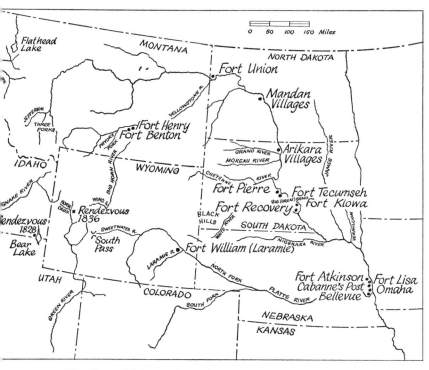

Northern Plains and Rocky Mountains, 1819–43

in the fur trade had taught him that *engagés* preferred to be paid in good pork, sugar, coffee, flour, and fresh or dried corn rather than in watered-down alcohol, so he kept the supply room filled with food and pampered the crops. Although corn production had been poor in 1833, both the corn and potato crops flourished the following year. By March, 1835, he had cleared and fenced approximately eighteen additional acres.[7] Healthy-looking cattle,

[7] Joshua Pilcher to Pierre Chouteau, Jr., June 16, 1833, and March 19, 1835, Chouteau MSS, MoSHi.

grazing near the post, supplied the garrison with dairy products, and swine, rooting in the woods, furnished pork to supplement game brought in by post hunters. Joshua supplied fresh food to traders, and competitors, moving up and down the Missouri River, and fed his visitors well.[8] Leclerc's spoiled flour and pork had been given to the Indians, who liked it in any condition.

In addition to the Indians and traders who frequented the post during 1833 and 1834, some travelers accepted Joshua's hospitality. Nathaniel J. Wyeth, an empire-builder interested in the fur trade and the northwestern fisheries, dropped by in September, 1833, on his way to St. Louis from the Indian country. Wyeth stayed at the post just long enough to renew his acquaintance with Joshua, whom he had met in St. Louis in the spring of 1832, and to enjoy his "utmost hospitality" and a tasty meal with "a good assortment of vegetables." Then, he continued downriver, supplied with flour, sugar, pepper, and salt from Joshua's storeroom.[9]

The following May, 1834, Joshua again "gave [Maximilian] a very cordial reception" and supplied him with "provisions from his store." After dinner the Prince roamed the surrounding hills observing the trees, shrubs, and birds. His companion, Bodmer, painted portraits of two of the most representative Indians amongst the Otoes, Missourias, Omahas, and Iowas at the post. "At nightfall" the artist and his royal patron "took leave of Mr. Pilcher" and boarded their boat for the night, "intending to proceed early the next morning." Maximilian, pleased with a gift from Joshua, "a very beautiful skin of a large dark brown wolf," regretted that he had to leave the post so quickly.[10] Later in the year a missionary, Samuel Allis, stopped at the post briefly to talk

[8] *Ibid.*, September 11, 1833, and February 2, 1834, *ibid.*; Maximilian, *Travels*, XXIV, 107.

[9] F. G. Young (ed.), *The Correspondence and Journals of Captain Nathaniel J. Wyeth 1831-6*, 218; Joshua Pilcher to Pierre Chouteau, Jr., September 23, 1833, Chouteau MSS, MoSHi.

[10] Maximilian, *Travels*, XXIV, 106–107.

to Joshua and "found the major [many of Joshua's friends referred to him by his rank in the Ree campaign] one of the most prompt, candid, and reliable gentlemen I have met with in the Indian country." Joshua promised John Dunbar, another missionary visitor, to help him with a mission to the Sioux. Dunbar thought that Joshua might become a valuable correspondent of the American Board of Commissioners of Foreign Missions, but Joshua did not take on this letter-writing task.[11]

Try as he might to treat his men fairly, only some of them liked him, others thoroughly disliked him, and he was forced to discipline a few employees, and to find replacements for those who deserted to the settlements downriver or simply ran off to live with the Indians. Joshua had inherited some personnel problems from his predecessor. He hired, as a "kind of domestic," a man whom Cabanné had allowed to perform odd jobs around the post for his keep during the summer, and was embarrassed because he was "neither one thing or another" and, generally, was incompetent.[12] Cholera hit Council Bluffs in the summer of 1833 and compounded Joshua's problems with his *engagés*, their families, and one "worthless ungrateful" man at Bellevue. Fortunately, Joshua saved most of the people stricken at his post because he "had a better stock of medicines" on hand (and medical training?) than

[11] Samuel Allis, "Forty Years among the Indians and on the Eastern Borders of Nebraska," *Transactions and Reports of the Nebraska State Historical Society,* Vol. II (1887), 161; the Diary of Marcus Whitman quoted in Archer Butler and Dorothy P. Hulbert, *Marcus Whitman, Crusader, Part One, 1802 to 1839,* 159. Young William Marshall Anderson, traveling in the West to recover from yellow fever, passed two days at this post in the pleasant company of Pilcher and Cabanné (he had returned to Council Bluffs from St. Louis) in September, 1834, and marveled at "one of the most remarkable natural curiosities I ever saw . . . [shown him] by Mr. Pilcher. . . . It was the skin of a deer, purely spotlessly white . . . great medicine [to the Indians]." Dale L. Morgan and Eleanor Towles Harris (eds.), *The Rocky Mountain Journals of William Marshall Anderson,* 210–11, 215.

[12] Joshua Pilcher to Pierre Chouteau, Jr., June 16, 1833, Chouteau MSS, MoSHi.

was available at Bellevue, where several died.[13] During July and August, he dashed back and forth between his post and Bellevue nursing the sick and dying with calomel and other preparations. He escaped the epidemic with only a slight infection, but felt "verry [*sic*] unsafe and . . . by no means well." Dougherty escaped death from the disease, although he was in "bad health," as Joshua reported to Chouteau, and lived temporarily at Cabanné's Post under Joshua's care. The epidemic lasted until cooler weather arrived in the fall.[14]

One man in particular disrupted life at the post during the winter of 1833. Louis Penault, a half-blood hunter, "deliberately shot" Louis Blay "through the heart with a rifle without any provocation" while drunk during a celebration on Christmas Day.[15] Joshua clapped Penault in irons until he could be sent downriver with the overland winter express to St. Louis. In the spring a lawyer investigated the murder at the post and may have taken depositions. Was Penault ever tried for the crime? The eminent fur trade historian, Hiram M. Chittenden, says that the American Fur Company, anxious to hide the fact that liquor was being sold at their posts, successfully prevented witnesses from descending the Missouri River to testify at the trial and won Penault's acquittal. However, since no citations or trial papers exist in the records of the federal court responsible in the Indian country, it is doubtful that Penault was ever brought before a court, much less tried for murder.[16]

Fortunately, most of the *engagés* at Cabanné's Post were loyal,

[13] *Ibid.*, December 18, 1833, *ibid.*; Maximilian, *Travels*, XXIV, 107.

[14] Joshua Pilcher to Pierre Chouteau, Jr., August 21 and September 11, 1833, Chouteau MSS, MoSHi.

[15] *Ibid.*, January 16, 1834, *ibid.*

[16] Hiram M. Chittenden, *Early Steamboat Navigation on the Missouri River: Life and Adventures of Joseph La Barge*, I, 42–44; Maximilian, *Travels*, XXIV, 106.

trustworthy individuals who troubled Joshua little if at all. One young man, Joseph La Barge, who wintered at the post in 1833–34, impressed Joshua as a "faithful active & enterprising" employee. They took their meals together—traditionally *engagés* did not eat with the bourgeois (chief trader)—and in May, 1834, because there was no position available at Cabanné's Post for a man of La Barge's abilities, Joshua recommended him for a clerkship on the upper Missouri. Despite Joshua's letter of recommendation to the company, he apparently viewed La Barge, at times, with mixed emotions—in February, 1834, for example, he referred to La Barge, in a letter to Chouteau, as a "worthless fellow." Joshua usually stuck to his opinions, good or bad, yet in this case he must have changed his mind later in the season.[17]

Between late spring, 1833, and March, 1835, when he accepted an appointment in the federal Indian Service, Joshua had seldom left the Council Bluffs area. For the first time in several years he had lived in one location for more than a few months. Many of his men and the men at Bellevue had Indian wives and families. Sometime in the late spring or early summer of 1833 he had taken a wife, possibly Cabanné's former "servant woman," who was the half-blood daughter of Michel Barada, a French trader, and an Omaha woman. Early in 1834 she gave birth to a son, John Pilcher. After she died of cholera the infant was taken to be raised by Big Elk, an Omaha chief. Apparently, Joshua showed little concern for the child, gave him far less attention than he gave the fur trade, and did not mention him in his will. The Omaha tribe never questioned John's parentage; Joshua was his father and Pilcher was his family name. John grew up on the Omaha reservation in eastern Nebraska, married Harriet Arlington, fathered

<hr />

[17] Joshua Pilcher to Pierre Chouteau, Jr., January 16 and February 2, 1834, and to Daniel Lamont, May 16, 1834, Chouteau MSS, MoSHi; Chittenden, *Early Steamboat Navigation*, I, 39.

ten children, and when he died in January, 1898, near Walthill, Nebraska, left dozens of descendants bearing the Pilcher name.[18]

The American Fur Company frequently used the term "Otto Outfit" to refer to Joshua's trade at Cabanné's Post because so much of the trade was with the neighboring Otoe Indians.[19] Unrestricted by the humorous name, Joshua traded regularly with Indians from several other friendly tribes who frequented the post and sent traders west to the Omahas and Pawnees, or east into Iowa; even upriver to the Sioux. The reports that he received from his traders in the field were not always reliable, and caused him to overestimate or underestimate returns and requisitions for goods and supplies at times. He preferred not to give credit to the Indians since they thought anything bought on credit was a present and would, if pressed for payment, take their furs and skins to another trader. But, on one occasion, in the early fall of 1833, he gave the Omahas powder and ball on credit as a bribe, to leave Cabanné's Post before they could exhaust his hospitality and eat up the corn crop.[20]

In addition to the daily routine of running Cabanné's Post and supervising traders at the Indian villages, Joshua exchanged information with traders at other company posts along the river and corresponded regularly with Chouteau in St. Louis. McKenzie, who was running a still at Fort Union to circumvent the federal

[18] "Death of Mrs. John Pilcher," *Nebraska History*, Vol. V (July, 1922), 49; Harriet L. Pilcher, "My Pioneer Life in Nebraska," n. d.; Tenth Census of the United States (1880), Soundex, Omaha Reservation, Neb., p. 426 (John Pilcher), Records of the Bureau of the Census, RG 29, NA; J. Sterling Morton, *Illustrated History of Nebraska*, I, 71 (n. 2); Notes from Manuscripts Relating to the Omaha Indians, Mrs. Roy M. Green, Lincoln, Nebraska. John Pilcher said he was born in 1833, instead of the more logical date, early 1834. Mrs. Green speculates that Joshua may have espoused more than one Indian woman.

[19] American Fur Company Ledger W and X, MoSHi.

[20] Joshua Pilcher to Pierre Chouteau, Jr., August 1, September 11, October 15 and 22, December 18, 1833, January 16 and July 7, 1834, and March 19, 1835, Chouteau MSS, MoSHi.

law prohibiting the transportation of liquor into Indian country, wrote Joshua late in 1833: "I hope you will be able to furnish me with a good supply of corn in the Spring or my wine vats will be idle."[21] Joshua liked McKenzie, and planted a bigger cornfield in 1834. Occasionally, when Joshua answered a letter from someone he disliked, he showed his bad temper. Within a month after he took over Cabanné's Post he wrote Chouteau telling him to write him in English, not in French.[22] Joshua did not read French and disliked and distrusted Chouteau's practice of sending directions to company posts in a foreign language. When Cabanné, in St. Louis, took offense at some of Joshua's statements written to Chouteau in the summer of 1833, Joshua defended himself, in words reminiscent of his quarrel with Austin and his battle with the bank, and so warned the company not to step on his toes: ". . . while my letters are open to the *criticism* of every gentleman—the man has yet to be born . . . who is to dictate the particular stile [*sic*] or phraseology of any communication I may think fit to make; or to restrain me in offering any suggestion which I may deem proper."[23]

Competition in the fur trade at Council Bluffs and in the surrounding country was light during Joshua's tenure at Cabanné's Post, and he instructed his traders in the field to hold to the exchange rate set at the post for pelts, but if an opposition trader offered more, he allowed his men to outbid the competition.[24] The greatest competition, in 1833, had come from the partnership of Ashley's former mountain man, Smith's partner for four years, William L. Sublette and Robert Campbell, the shrewd Scot trader and investor. Sublette and Campbell competed at many choice locations along the Missouri River, before they pulled back from the river, in the spring of 1834, to concentrate on the mountain

[21] Kenneth McKenzie to Joshua Pilcher, December 16, 1833, Ft. Union LB, October 29, 1833–December 10, 1835, *ibid.*

[22] Joshua Pilcher to Pierre Chouteau, Jr., June 16, 1833, *ibid.*

[23] *Ibid.*, August 1, 1833, *ibid.*

[24] *Ibid.*, October 15, 1833, and May 15, 1834, *ibid.*

fur trade. Competition was less irritating to Joshua, however, than the responsibility circumstances thrust upon him for the *engagés* who had been associated with Fontenelle in his trading ventures for the company since 1828. Joshua thought one former Fontenelle man was "partially *insane*" and he may have lost $100 to the same "worthless ungreatful [*sic*] fellow."[25]

During his service at the post, changes taking place in federal Indian policy were shaping the outline of Joshua's career for the next seven years. In 1834 the Congress, after many years of discussion, had finally reorganized the Indian service, and now the time was ripe for Joshua to renew pressure on the Jackson administration for an agency job. In November somebody at Council Bluffs, it could have been Joshua himself, wrote to Secretary of War Cass recommending Joshua for appointment as Sioux sub-agent.[26] Either Joshua knew that Jonathan L. Bean, the Sioux sub-agent, planned to resign and timed the application accordingly, or luck favored him and the letter reached the War Department at the right moment. In mid-February, 1835, Bean resigned to seek a better-paying job, and on either March 4 or 5— the records disagree—Joshua was appointed sub-agent for a "portion of the Sioux . . . High up [the] Missouri" at an annual salary of $750.[27] The sub-agency, located at Fort Lookout, just below Big (Great) Bend on the Missouri River, near the site of old Fort Recovery, served the Indians—mostly Sioux—who lived in a vast rectangular section bounded on the east by the Missouri River,

[25] *Ibid.*, October 15 and December 18, 1833, *ibid.*

[26] Letter of Application dated November 1, 1834, Register of Letters Received by the Secretary of War, RG 107, NA.

[27] J. L. Bean to Lewis Cass, February 15, 1835, LR, OIA, RG 75, NA; "Report From the Secretary of War, with annual List of Officers and other persons engaged in the Indian Department," 24 Cong., 1 sess., *SD No. 109*, p. 3; "A List of the Names of Persons Employed in the Indian Department during the Year 1836, and the Pay and Salary of Each," 24 Cong., 2 sess., *HED No. 141*, p. 5.

on the west by the Black Hills, on the north by the Moreau River, and on the south by the Niobrara River and the North Fork of the Platte. Joshua complained to Clark that the sub-agency stood at an inconvenient point on the extreme eastern edge of the rectangle, but advised the Indian Office not to move it until "the policy of the government is more fully developed respecting the removal of Indians from the east and the effect of the location made by those Indians [is] ascertained."[28]

Joshua received notice of his appointment in April, but delayed making the trip from Council Bluffs to St. Louis to post bond, because the Indian annuity payment, for the first six months of 1835 for his sub-agency, was expected to arrive any day. While he waited at Council Bluffs he met the Reverend Samuel Parker, on his way west to convert the Indians in Oregon, and "in several interviews" told the missionary about the Sioux and gave him his candid opinion that "there would be no difficulty in sending missionaries among them provided . . . ," Joshua wisely added, the missionaries "go with them where they go—learn their language, and gradually use their influence to have them settle down and cultivate the soil."[29]

On June 10 an American Fur Company steamboat with supplies, for the upper Missouri posts, and the annuities, finally reached Council Bluffs. The captain handed Joshua a packet of printed regulations from the Indian Office outlining proper procedure in the distribution of Indian annuities. According to the regulations, as Joshua understood them, normally distribution was made by army officers unless the Indian agency was located far from an army post. In that instance, the agent or sub-agent was directly responsible for giving out the annuities. Since his sub-

[28] Joshua Pilcher to William Clark, July 21, 1835, and to Carey A. Harris, January 23, 1837, LR, OIA, RG 75, NA.
[29] Samuel Parker to D. Greene, June 9, 1835, and Parker's Report, quoted in Hulbert and Hulbert, *Whitman*, 85–86, 93.

agency was hundreds of miles from the nearest military post and he had received no contrary instructions from Fort Leavenworth, he assumed that the annuities were consigned to him. He boarded the steamboat and steamed upriver along with the goods and money to his new sub-agency.[30]

At the Big Bend he found a mass of starving Indians waiting for the overdue annuities. Regardless of their plight, they had to wait thirteen days longer, until all the scattered tribesmen assigned to the sub-agency had come in from the plains. On July 5, still without contrary instructions from the Indian Office or Fort Leavenworth, he distributed the annuities and counseled with the chiefs of the Indian bands assembled there. Two weeks later an army lieutenant turned up at the sub-agency to supervise distribution. Joshua, embarrassed by the situation, stuck to his interpretation of the regulations and wrote the Commissioner of Indian Affairs requesting that he be clearly given, for reasons of safety and efficiency, all annuity distribution power at his sub-agency. He also asked the Indian Office to allot him money to buy corn to feed the Indians whenever they gathered at the sub-agency to wait for annuities. The army lieutenant returned to his superiors at Fort Leavenworth to explain the conflict in authority over annuities and became entangled in a mountain of red tape before he extricated himself from the annuity venture. The army, in response to all of this confusion, recommended to the Indian Office that annuity-distribution duties be turned over entirely to Indian agents.[31]

Between July 5, annuity distribution day, and July 18, when the army officer arrived at the Big Bend, Joshua had visited several trading posts and had given presents to the Indians in the villages.

---

[30] Joshua Pilcher to J. B. Brant, October 6, 1835, and William Clark to Elbert Herring, May 15, 1835, LR, OIA, RG 75, NA.

[31] *Ibid.*; Joshua Pilcher to Elbert Herring, August 25, 1835, and G. H. Crossman to Elbert Herring, August 5 and 20, 1835, *ibid.*

He reported to Clark that approximately 14,000 Sioux lived under the jurisdiction of the sub-agency and that, owing to careful supervision by the former agent, J. L. Bean, the sub-agency buildings were in good condition and the smithshop was of great service to the Indians.[32] He was short of help, and closed the smithey during the summer. The blacksmith and his striker were put to work repairing buildings, cutting and hauling wood, and making charcoal for the winter. Although no interpreter was assigned to the post and there was no provision for one, Joshua decided that he needed one and hired Jean Baptiste Dorion at a salary of $480 a year. He explained to Clark that the amount was high because he had to compete with the traders for competent employees and Dorion was worth every penny of the salary since he knew three or four languages. Clark endorsed Joshua's action in a letter to the Commissioner of Indian Affairs and requested the Indian Office to allot money for the interpreter's salary. Joshua also told Clark: it might be impossible for him to comply at all times with all the regulations of the Indian Office because his sub-agency was so remote from civilization that instructions from Washington and St. Louis took weeks, even months, to reach the Big Bend.[33]

By early August, Joshua had completed the first phase of his work at the Big Bend. His employees were renovating the sub-agency according to his plans; he had hired an interpreter, despite regulations to the contrary; he, rather than an army officer, had delivered the annuities to the Sioux; he had notified the Indian Office that the Sioux preferred goods instead of money as annuities, because money slipped through their fingers into the pockets of the traders. In addition, he had asked Clark to allow him to hire a farmer, to teach the Indians something about agriculture, and to

[32] Joshua Pilcher to William Clark, July 18, 1835, *ibid.*
[33] *Ibid.*, July 1, 1835, *ibid.*; Joshua Pilcher to Elbert Herring, August 25, 1835; William Clark to Elbert Herring, August 1, 1835; and Abstract of Sioux sub-agency Employees as of September 30, 1835, *ibid.*

buy two horses or oxen to use as sub-agency draught animals. The Sioux were peaceful, so Joshua, taking advantage of the lull afforded by the unusually good Indian disposition, returned to St. Louis to post bond on his commission and look into details of sub-agency business.[34] He reached St. Louis on or shortly before August 26, passed a few busy weeks in the city, filed a $1,000 bond, and returned to the Big Bend in October to prepare his sub-agency for the coming winter.

Meanwhile, a small band of Ponca Indians, who had formerly lived at the mouth of the Niobrara River in Dougherty's agency, were transferred to Joshua's jurisdiction. He accepted the "added burden" because the Poncas were rapidly being killed off by the Pawnees. Dorion spoke the Ponca language, and Joshua reminded the Indian Office that he was saving the government money by not hiring a second interpreter and emphasized repeatedly that he was responsible for a greater number of Indians than any other agent and that his salary was inadequate.[35] He was particularly angry at the Indian Office when he learned, before leaving St. Louis, that the Secretary of War had disallowed his request for $180, additional money to pay his interpreter. He refused to discharge Dorion or to pay his salary from his own pocket; instead, he appealed to the Congress for relief.[36]

Joshua had more friends in Congress than in the War Department and the Indian Office, still smarting over the Ree campaign. In January, 1836, in response to his earlier appeal the House Committee on Indian Affairs had reported favorably on a relief bill. Six months later, the Congress passed a relief act, approved

[34] Joshua Pilcher to Elbert Herring, July 7, 1835, and to William Clark, August 18, 1835, *ibid*.

[35] John Dougherty to William Clark, August 20, 1835; Joshua Pilcher to William Clark, August 26, 1835, and to D. Kurtz, August 31, 1835; and Abstract of Indians of the Sioux sub-agency furnished on October 5, 1835, *ibid*.

[36] Joshua Pilcher to D. Kurtz, August 31, 1835, *ibid*.; Elbert Herring to Joshua Pilcher, September 17, 1835, LS, OIA, RG 75, NA.

July 1, 1836, authorizing the Secretary of War "to allow Joshua Pitcher [*sic*] the sum of one hundred dollars in the settlement of his accounts." The sum authorized reimbursed Joshua for the money he had advanced to Dorion's salary—Clark had paid the greater part of the interpreter's salary from contingent funds— for the period July 1, 1835 to July 1, 1836. Joshua directed the government to pay the money to Edward Brooks, a St. Louis druggist, who had married into the Riddick family. Brooks apparently paid the money to one or more of Joshua's creditors, to settle some of the Missouri Fur Company debts still outstanding.[37]

His first annual report on conditions in his sub-agency, sent the Indian Office in October, 1835, covered the entire scope of the operation. Generally he was optimistic about the Sioux in his jurisdiction; they had been peaceful; no liquor had reached them during that summer. Although most of them continued to subsist upon buffalo, a few Yanktons and Santees were growing corn at the mouth of the Vermillion River: they had urged him to move the blacksmith shop down near their corn patches, but Joshua, dubious that many of the Sioux would settle at the Vermillion, had told the Indians he would move the shop only if a sizable Indian settlement grew up there. Contrary to his remarks to Samuel Parker earlier in the year, he now judged that missionaries to the Sioux would do little good as long as the Indians were nomadic. He also noted that all attempts to educate Indian children within the sub-agency had failed and recommended that henceforth, all treaty funds for education be used to support Sioux children who would be sent to the Choctaw Academy, sponsored by Representative Richard M. Johnson, at Great Crossing, Kentucky. Two Yankton children were already attending the school, and the

---

[37] Peters (ed.), *Statutes at Large*, VI, Chap. CCXLVII; File 20910, RICC, RG 279, NA; Second Auditor to George Thomas, December 10, 1836, LB No. 20, p. 451, Sec. A, USGAO, RG 217, NA; House Committee on Indian Affairs, Report No. 230 (Joshua Pilcher), January 27, 1836, Records of the United States House of Representatives, RG 233, NA.

Yankton chiefs had offered to send more children to the institution and to contribute their share of the education fund to the school.[38]

Joshua remained at his post until the following March when he visited St. Louis briefly to readjust his debts once again and to learn what arrangements were being made by the Indian Office for the delivery of annuities to the Sioux later in the season.[39] By mid-May he was again at the Big Bend, where he found peace threatened by roving bands of Sioux from Minnesota. No major outbreak occurred, however, and he spent the late spring and early summer putting the sub-agency in better order. Since Dorion was too busy with the Sioux to act as interpreter for the Ponca, Joshua changed his mind about a second interpreter, appointed one for the Ponca, and asked Clark to pay the new interpreter's salary. Clark allowed $100 for the year 1836–37, but the Indian Office refused to certify a larger amount.[40] The government agreed to appoint a farmer, as Joshua had requested, to supervise the Sioux agricultural settlement on the Vermillion. Although agricultural implements and supplies, promised by the government late in 1835, were slow in reaching the Vermillion, the farmer succeeded "tolerably well," in Joshua's words, in teaching corn culture to about twenty-five families of Yankton and Santee Sioux at the Vermillion.[41] In July, 1836, the Indian Office also consented to another of Joshua's requests. He was permitted to make annuity payments without military supervision. Another of his suggestions of 1835, that the Indian Office allow him to buy corn for the

38 Joshua Pilcher to William Clark, October 6, 1835, and to Elbert Herring, July 7, 1835, LR, OIA, RG 75, NA.

39 Joshua Pilcher to Ramsay Crooks, March 24, 1836, American Fur Company Papers, NHi.

40 Joshua Pilcher to William Clark, May 15, 1836; William Clark to Elbert Herring, July 11, 1836, and to C. A. Harris, August 18, 1836; and Abstract of Employees Sioux sub-agency for the Year Ending September 30, 1836, LR, OIA, RG 75, NA.

41 Joshua Pilcher to Elbert Herring, October 3, 1836, and J. B. Brant to Elbert Herring, April 13, 1836, *ibid.*

Carlton House.

Bellevue, from a painting by Charles Bodmer in Maximilian's *Travels*.

Sioux, had been approved in time for the annuity payment of 1836.[42] By following one path or another, direct or devious, Joshua won his contests with the Indian Office while he was sub-agent to the Sioux.

In June, 1836, under orders from the Indian Office, he left the Big Bend on a three-month trip to visit the wandering tribes in his sub-agency, west of the Missouri River. He hired a messenger to contact tribes along the way and, probably, brought along one of the two interpreters assigned to his sub-agency. Joshua reported to the Indian Office in October, after he returned to the Big Bend, that he saw no material change in the tribes during his summer journey—conditions amongst the Indians were about the same as in 1835.[43] In his report he did not mention that he had served the American Fur Company as well as the government during the summer. The story is difficult to piece together because the company said little about its business deals and made rather complex agreements with its associates. Apparently, Chouteau had asked Joshua to investigate the activities of Fontenelle, Fitzpatrick & Company (Fontenelle, Thomas Fitzpatrick, Jim Bridger, Milton Sublette, and Drips) and, if possible, buy them out for the American Fur Company. Fontenelle and his partners, loosely tied to Chouteau, were toying with the idea of opposing his company and were co-operating with the rival firm of Sublette and Campbell.[44] In mid-June, Joshua reached Fort William at the confluence of the Laramie and North Platte rivers. He wrote Chouteau that "everything I see and hear, admonishes me to move with caution and prudence." Conditions there were unfavorable to the com-

[42] Joshua Pilcher to C. A. Harris, October 1, 1836, *ibid.*; C. A. Harris to Joshua Pilcher, July 16, 1836, LS, OIA, RG 75, NA.

[43] Joshua Pilcher to C. A. Harris, October 3, 1836, and Abstract of Requisitions drawn by Joshua Pilcher as sub-agent for the Sioux . . . for the quarter ending September 30, 1836, LR, OIA, RG 75, NA.

[44] William L. Sublette was Robert Campbell's partner. His brothers Milton, Andrew, Pinckney, and Solomon were also active in the fur trade.

pany: if only Chouteau's "eyes could reach" the post! Joshua also remarked that his horses were in poor condition, better ones were unavailable, and he was anxious to reach the summer rendezvous; he hoped to have information of "great importance" for the company by early August; and everything would depend upon the arrangements to be made at the coming rendezvous.[45]

At Fort William, about June 21, Joshua joined the annual American Fur Company supply caravan from the east and accompanied it west across Wyoming to the rendezvous at Horse Creek on Green River.[46] He "rode a fine white mule," evidently he had bartered one of his poor horses for a better mount at the fort, and impressed a party of Oregon missionaries, attached to the caravan, with his gentlemanly "conversation and deportment" and "mountain style ... fine buckskin coat trimmed with red cloth and porcupine quills, fine red shirt, nice buckskin pants, and moccasins tinged and nicely trimmed." In addition to the fur traders and the missionary party, notably the Reverend Dr. Marcus Whitman and the Reverend Henry H. Spalding and their wives; a British visitor, Sir William Drummond Stewart, traveled with the pack train in a motley caravan of cart, wagon, and livestock. The journey from Fort William to Green River proved quite a social success for everyone attached to the train. Joshua played the gallant courtier to the missionary ladies successfully until in his enthusiasm he lost his balance one day and "dropped out of sight" with his mule into a clay pit. Man and mule emerged covered with mud, but he held his temper "and joined in the jokes on the occasion."[47]

45 Joshua Pilcher to Pierre Chouteau, Jr., June 21, 1836, and to the Gentlemen at Ft. Pierre, June 21, 1836, Chouteau MSS, MoSHi.

46 L. Crawford to Pierre Chouteau, Jr., June 29, 1836, *ibid.*

47 William Henry Gray, *A History of Oregon, 1792–1849,* 116–23. The description of Joshua bound for the rendezvous is the best ever written. We have no accurate physical description of him and, unfortunately, no painting, sketch, daguerreotype, or other likeness.

At the rendezvous in the verdant Green River Valley, Joshua and Stewart waited upon the ladies and assured them that they were safe from the hundreds of Indians "hooting and yelling" in the camp. Joshua negotiated with Fontenelle, Fitzpatrick and Company and arranged for the American Fur Company to buy them out.[48] At the rendezvous he also met two Hudson's Bay Company traders, John L. McLeod and Thomas McKay, who had brought British merchandise to sell at the encampment. The American traders treated them "very coolly, saying [they were] intruding on their territory," but Joshua "remembered the Politeness that had been shewn him in the Columbia, and at Red River . . . immediately interfered, and stoped [sic] their proceedings."[49] Before the missionaries left the rendezvous for Oregon, he assured Dr. Whitman that, although missionaries could not work successfully with nomadic tribes, they could live safely with settled Indians, such as the Sioux farmers on the Vermillion, and said that missionaries should be allowed to use Indian agency buildings belonging to the federal government.

When the rendezvous broke up, before the end of July, Joshua headed east and slowly made his way back to the Big Bend where he compiled a brief annual report for the Indian Office and applied to Clark for a leave of absence to attend to private business in St. Louis.[50] When Clark replied that he lacked the power to grant a leave, Joshua appealed directly to the Indian Office, and went down the Missouri River to Fort Leavenworth. The Indian Office delayed answering his letter until mid-December and, while he waited for approval of his leave application at the fort, Clark

[48] Marcus Whitman to Samuel Parker, September 18, 1836, and to Unknown, July 16, 1836, quoted in Hulbert and Hulbert, *Whitman*, 210, 230–31.

[49] John McLoughlin to the Governor, Deputy Governor, and Committee Hudson's Bay Company, October 31, 1837, quoted in E. E. Rich (ed.), *The Letters of John McLoughlin From Fort Vancouver to the Governor and Committee First Series, 1825–38*, 209.

[50] Joshua Pilcher to C. A. Harris, October 3, 1836, LR, OIA, RG 75, NA.

ordered him upriver with Dougherty on "verry [sic] important business."[51] At Bellevue they met with chiefs representing the Otoe, Missouri, Omaha, Yankton, and Santee tribes, who claimed a triangular piece of land wedged between the state of Missouri and the Missouri River. On October 15 the Indians ceded, by convention, the "beautiful . . . valuable" tract, as Joshua described it, to the United States for presents (merchandise) valued at $4,520, five hundred bushels of corn to be delivered in the spring, and, to the Omahas, promises of agricultural assistance.[52] The land, known as the Platte Purchase, was a bargain at any price—a steal at the price paid—although the Reverend Moses Merrill, a missionary to the Otoes who apparently knew little about land values, took the opposite view and confided to his diary his praise "to the Lord who put into the hearts of the agents" (Dougherty and Joshua) the humane provisions of the treaty![53] Joshua, who knew good land when he saw it, wrote to his friends at Fort Pierre, the American Fur Company post north of the Big Bend, that he hoped "to make something out of the land ceded." But his plans were bigger than his purse; he never invested in Platte Purchase land.[54]

When the council ended at Bellevue, Joshua went to St. Louis for medical attention. He had not received authorized leave from

[51] C. A. Harris to Joshua Pilcher, December 14, 1836, LS, OIA, RG 75, NA; Joshua Pilcher to Jacob Halsey or P. D. Papin, October 18, 1836, Chouteau MSS, MoSHi.

[52] John Dougherty and Joshua Pilcher to William Clark, October 15, 1836, LR, OIA, RG 75, NA; Treaty at Bellevue, October 15, 1836, with the Otoes, Missouries, Omahawas, Yancton and Santees, Clark MSS, Vol. 1, pp. 258–61, KHi; Berlin B. Chapman, *The Otoes and the Missourias*, 31–32.

[53] "Extracts from the Diary of Rev. Moses Merrill, a Missionary to the Otoe Indians from 1832 to 1840," *Transactions and Reports of the Nebraska Historical Society*, Vol. IV (1892), 117.

[54] Joshua Pilcher to Jacob Halsey or P. D. Papin, October 18, 1836, Chouteau MSS, MoSHi. In a letter to the same men, dated December 16, 1836, Joshua used the term "Ft. Laremy" to refer to Fort William (Fort Lucien Laramie). Thus, he was one of the first individuals to apply the name Laramie to the important post at the junction of the Laramie and North Platte rivers.

the Indian Office, but he was exhausted from his summer journey, especially from the time he had spent scouring the plains in search of the Oglala Sioux, from the hard work at the treaty council, and from his efforts in behalf of Chouteau. In St. Louis his "disease," whatever it was, caught up with him late in the fall, and he was bedridden from Christmas time until March, 1837. On January 12 he received word from the Indian Office that he had been granted a sixty-day leave, retroactive to the fall, but by the end of the month his leave had elapsed and his "little pay" was running out. He left his sickroom for the first time on March 21, still feeling in "very bad health," determined to return as soon as possible to duty on the upper Missouri.[55]

[55] Joshua Pilcher to C. A. Harris, January 23 and March 23, 1837, LR, OIA, RG 75, NA.

AGENT TO THE SIOUX,
CHEYENNES, AND PONCAS

T WO WEEKS before Joshua got up from his sick bed President Van Buren nominated him Indian agent to the Sioux, Cheyenne, and Ponca Indians. The Senate Committee on Indian Affairs favorably endorsed the recommendation and, on March 8, the upper house consented to the President's selection. Benton informed Joshua of the good news, and at the end of the month Secretary of War Joel R. Poinsett sent his new commission. He accepted it immediately after he received it in St. Louis, on April 14, and filed bond of $2,000 two days later. Then he left hurriedly on the American Fur Company steamboat *St. Peter's* for the upper Missouri to resume his duties at the Big Bend at a salary double his former sub-agent pay. John Sanford, now employed by Chouteau, sent Joshua's bond to the Indian Office, but it had been executed improperly and the Commissioner returned it to Joshua to be redone. When Joshua submitted the bond in proper form, he complained, in Pilcherian fashion, that his pay as agent commenced on the day of his commission, March 31, and not on the date in mid-April when he accepted the appointment. But Indian Commissioner Carey A. Harris was unruffled by Joshua's protest; by then the Indian Office was used to his testiness.[1]

Joshua's prestige in the Indian service increased with his ap-

[1] *Journal of The Executive Proceedings of the Senate*, V, 19–20, 22; Joshua Pilcher to C. A. Harris, March 23, April 16, and October 18, 1837, and to Joel R. Poinsett, April 16, 1837, and Joshua Pilcher's Bond with Note Attached, April 16, 1837, LR, OIA, RG 75, NA; C. A. Harris to Joshua Pilcher, March 31, and May 18, 1837, and Joel R. Poinsett to Joshua Pilcher, March 31, 1837, LS, OIA, RG 75, NA. See Peters (ed.), *Statutes at Large*, V, 158–63, for the Indian Appropriation Act of March 3, 1837, in which a new Indian agency was created for the upper Missouri, replacing the old sub-agency.

pointment to the Sioux Agency. The old sub-agent's job was abolished: the positions of agent and sub-agent were consolidated into one, and he was given some formal jurisdiction over the Cheyennes and Poncas. The number of square miles under his supervision remained unchanged, and he was assured that Clark, in St. Louis, was his immediate superior, not Henry Dodge, the new governor and superintendent of Indian affairs of Wisconsin Territory, to whom Joshua was mistakenly assigned by the Indian Office in the summer of 1836. By early June, Joshua was again at the Big Bend supervising the distribution of annuity goods to the Sioux and the work of his agency employees. The farmer, paid through the agricultural fund of the Indian Office, with only a little Indian help, since most of the tribesmen were short of food and had gone hunting, had cleared, plowed, and planted fifteen to eighteen acres near the agency and, at least, one additional field twenty miles farther south at the mouth of White River. Joshua's employees—two interpreters, a blacksmith, a striker, and a farmer—seemed to be dependable, hard-working men who carried out their duties to the critical agent's satisfaction. The Indian Office had finally allowed Joshua to buy horses for the agency farmer, nearly thirty Indian families had settled below the agency, and Joshua hoped to have sufficient funds from the Indian Office in 1838 to put most of his agency Indians to work on the land.[2]

In contrast to the relatively well-ordered serene life at the Sioux Agency, conditions were deteriorating rapidly among the Indians living elsewhere along the Missouri River below and above the Big Bend. Smallpox, carried upriver on the *St. Peter's,* invaded the Missouri Valley, and Joshua had warned the Sioux to stay away from the river and the trading posts for the summer. To stricken Indians he administered salts, castor oil, and any other drug or remedy handy to fight smallpox with little success, and he

---

[2] Joshua Pilcher to William Clark, June 10, and September 5, 1837, and Abstract of Joshua Pilcher's Requisitions for the Quarter Ending June 30, 1837, LR, OIA, RG 75, NA.

feared all the tribes between the Platte and the Yellowstone would catch the disease. Most of them did. In a few years entire villages were decimated, and Indians along the upper Missouri died by the thousands. Most of the white traders and Indian agency employees survived the smallpox, but the fur trade was stunned, and the problems of Indian administration multiplied.[3]

In the midst of the epidemic, Joshua recruited an Indian delegation to visit the Great White Father. In April, before he left St. Louis for the Indian country, Clark, under instruction of the Indian Office, had ordered him to gather as many as ten chiefs and leading men from the Yankton and Santee Sioux and conduct them to Washington by October 1. Clark also instructed Dougherty to assemble a small group of Sac and Fox Indians from the Missouri Valley and to have them at Fort Leavenworth by August 15 ready to join Joshua as he descended the river with the Sioux. Andrew S. Hughes, of the Ioway Agency, who had been told to have four Ioway chiefs ready to join the delegation, was humiliated to learn that Joshua was to lead them.[4] The two men had disliked each other because Joshua had accused Hughes during the Black Hawk War of spreading unfounded rumors along the Iowa-Illinois frontier. Hughes wrote asking Vice-President Johnson to influence Commissioner Harris to order him, rather than Joshua, to conduct the Ioway chiefs to see the President. Hughes noted that the Ioway chiefs had expressed anxiety in council because he was not to lead them east and volunteered to pay his own expenses on the trip. Vice-President Johnson asked Commissioner Harris, "as a particular personal favor," to permit Hughes to lead the Ioways to Washington, but the Commissioner refused to give in and the Ioway chiefs went east with Joshua.[5]

[3] Joshua Pilcher to William Clark, June 10, and July 1, 1837, *ibid.*; Joshua Pilcher to Jacob Halsey or P. D. Papin, May 30, 1837, Chouteau MSS, MoSHi.

[4] George Maguire to C. A. Harris, May 10, 1837, and William Clark to Andrew S. Hughes, April 15, 1837, LR, OIA, RG 75, NA.

[5] Andrew S. Hughes to Vice-President Richard Johnson, June 30, 1837, *ibid.*

At the Big Bend Joshua easily collected a Sioux delegation early in June, but as smallpox spread along the Missouri Valley, he grew more and more apprehensive lest the epidemic disrupt his timetable. His fears were justified; smallpox hit the delegation. Some of the chiefs died, and others fled from the valley into the plains. He recruited substitutes immediately and, in the first week in July, took them downriver to Fort Leavenworth, where he made arrangements for assembling the delegation. He estimated that it would cost the government $5,000 for him to conduct the delegation of Sioux, Sac and Foxes, and Ioways to and from the East, but he assured the Indian Office he would adhere rigidly to the Commissioner's plea for economy and admitted that his estimate was largely guesswork.[6] He had proposed, early in May, that the government also invite an Omaha Indian delegation to see the President. They "might easily be induced to dispose of a part of their country . . . should it be considered desirable to obtain it," Clark's secretary wrote the Commissioner. The Indian Office agreed to this, and Commissioner Harris ordered Dougherty to bring a delegation of Otoes, Omahas, and Pawnees to Washington in the fall. When Joshua heard the news, he immediately volunteered to save the treasury money by attaching Dougherty's delegation to his party. If the government wished, he would lead the entire group of Sioux, Sac and Foxes, Ioways, Otoes, Omahas, and Pawnees to the East. Dougherty shrewdly parried Joshua's much-too-generous offer—clearly, his friendly adversary wished to monopolize the limelight and to make political hay in the capital—and arranged to lead his Indians east in November.[7]

[6] Joshua Pilcher to William Clark, June 10, and July 1, 1837, and to George Maguire, August 17, 1837, and George Maguire to C. A. Harris, July 14, 1837, *ibid.*; Joshua Pilcher to Jacob Halsey or P. D. Papin, May 30, 1837, Chouteau MSS, MoSHi.

[7] Joshua Pilcher to George Maguire, August 17, 1837, and to John Dougherty, August 17, 1837; George Maguire to C. A. Harris, May 10, 1837; and John Dougherty to C. A. Harris, November, 1837, LR, OIA, RG 75, NA.

Joshua remained in the Fort Leavenworth area over a month making preparations for the grand tour to the East. Other Indian delegations, notably one composed of Sac and Foxes of the Mississippi, led by Black Hawk and Keokuk, were also going to Washington to meet the President and hoped to settle old intertribal differences there. Joshua was anxious to impress the administration with an outstanding Indian delegation, to curry favor with the press, in competition with the other delegations for newspaper coverage, and to further his own career in the Indian service. On July 19 he boarded the steamboat *Kansas* for a short upriver trip to the Blacksnake Hills to meet the Yankton Sioux delegates—the Santee delegates had died. A few days later, unable to replace the Santees, he returned to Fort Leavenworth with the Yanktons. He sent some of the Sioux to St. Louis, but kept some with him. When the Sac and Foxes and Ioways joined the party in mid-August, he escorted his charges approximately thirty miles to Liberty Landing, where he bought beef, bacon, and corn for them and waited for transportation down the Missouri on the riverboat *Pirate*. On August 22 they landed in St. Louis and the entire delegation had been assembled.

Joshua bought presents, from Chouteau and Henry Shaw, for the nine or ten (the figures vary) Yankton Sioux, two Foxes, two Sacs, and four Ioways, and gave final instructions to his three interpreters and Charles Brazeau, his assistant in charge of the delegation.[8]

Joshua booked passage on the steamboat *Irene* for Cincinnati and handed in his annual report to Clark. On September 7 he led the delegation aboard the boat and steamed away from St. Louis.[9]

[8] George Maguire to C. A. Harris, August 26, 1837, *ibid*. Unless otherwise indicated, the dates of Joshua's itinerary on the round trip between St. Louis and the East are taken from File 2761, RICC, RG 279, NA.

[9] George Maguire to C. A. Harris, September 7, 1837, and Joshua Pilcher's Annual Report to the Commissioner of Indian Affairs, September 5, 1837, LR, OIA, RG 75, NA.

Then on September 12, the party changed boats in Cincinnati and continued on to Pittsburgh aboard the *Girard*. The boat made "a short tarry" at the wharf in Wheeling. It tarried just enough time for a few chiefs and an interpreter to climb a hill overlooking the town. The townspeople stared, the local newspaper printed an account of the hill-climbing red men, and the story spread east. Late Saturday evening, September 16, or early the following morning, they disembarked in Pittsburgh and passed a relatively quiet week end secluded in a downtown hotel.[10] Monday morning, the Indians boarded another remarkable means of transportation. They sailed across Pennsylvania in a canalboat through dozens of ingenious canal locks and rode up and down the inclined planes of the Pennsylvania Portage and Canal System, passing through Johnstown, Hollidaysburg, and Columbia. By September 23 they were in Philadelphia, and the following Monday they moved on to Baltimore. By the middle of the week, September 26 or 27, they reached Washington.

A "fierce-looking, stout and able-bodied" Sioux delegation from the upper Mississippi, "carrying . . . their bows and arrows, tomahawks and pikes," had preceded Joshua and his Indians to the capital and were meeting, almost daily, with representatives of the government in Dr. James Laurie's Presbyterian church on F Street.[11] Spectators crowded into the building to gawk at the Indians and the public officials, seated on a carpeted platform built below the pulpit, and listen to whatever snatches of the council the Van Buren administration wished to be heard in public. The *Morning Courier and New-York Enquirer* interpreted the treaty-making as "a very clever *ruse* in the administration to get up their Indian shows and exhibitions during the Extra Session [of

---

[10] The Pittsburgh *Advocate*, September 19, 1837, quoted in the *Daily National Intelligencer* (Washington), September 23, 1837; The Wheeling *Gazette*, no date given, quoted in the Philadelphia *Pennsylvanian*, September 25, 1837.

[11] *Daily National Intelligencer* (Washington), September 18 and 23, 1837.

Congress], to excite public curiosity, and then the attendance on the debates of Congress" concerning banking and land, both key issues in the new Van Buren regime. Perhaps the New York newspaper was correct. The sideshow filled the pews, aisles, galleries, doors, and windows of the church with eager onlookers whenever the council assembled.[12]

Joshua, the "little chief," the Indians called him, led his delegation of Sioux, Sac and Foxes, and Ioways to the church for the first time on Thursday morning, September 28. They sat on the platform to the left of Secretary of War Poinsett, and impressed the audience with their robust, fierce appearance. When the council adjourned for the day, Joshua took the Indians to the War Department, where Major General Alexander Macomb, commander-in-chief of the army, received them, then led them to see President Van Buren. Apparently, the meeting between the Great White Father and his red-skinned children was a social success, although the superstitious Indians refused to sit for the portraits wanted by the War Department. On Friday, September 29, the Minnesota Sioux signed a treaty with the government.

Saturday evening, all of the Indians in Washington attended the theater. The Minnesota Sioux, some outfitted by the government in military frock coats adorned with epaulettes, others in new blankets and leggings, sat in the parquet. Joshua's delegation sat to the left of the stage. When the leading lady appeared and moved about on the stage, a young Yankton chief, delighted by the performance, jumped up and threw his war cap at her feet. She fastened it to her costume, as if counting coup, and the other Indians joined the performance; an old Sac chief tossed in his war cap; a young Yankton brave contributed a white wolf robe; another Yankton chief gave her a "richly ornamented" buffalo robe; and another Yankton brave presented a second buffalo robe.

[12] *Morning Courier and New-York Enquirer* (New York City), October 23, 1837; *Daily National Intelligencer* (Washington), September 25 and 26, 1837.

The actress thanked them through an interpreter and handed each of the Indians an ostrich plume from her headdress. As she left the stage, "she spread over her brow [a] splendid war cap of eagle feathers, producing a most magical effect." The Indians wore her ostrich plumes in their war caps proudly when they paraded along Pennsylvania Avenue three days later.[13]

Between sessions of the Indian council Joshua visited friends in the administration and Congress and lobbied successfully for his pet projects. Some of the Indians in his agency, who had settled near the mouth of White River, wanted him to move the Sioux agency to a new location closer to their settlement. He favored moving, but had not decided upon a new site for the agency and needed Indian Office approval before he could transfer it to another location. While in Washington, he explained the situation to Commissioner Harris, who authorized him to select a new site for the agency. To defray moving costs, money was set aside in the Yankton Treaty signed on October 21. He also requested and received permission to visit, if he wished, the Choctaw Academy, at Great Crossing, Kentucky, on the way home from the capital. One of the two Yankton Sioux boys attending the academy had died and the other one was lonely, despondent, and anxious to see his parents. Since this boy's father was one of Joshua's delegation, Commissioner Harris told Joshua to take him to see his son in Kentucky and persuade the boy to remain in school.[14]

Preliminary meetings in Dr. Laurie's church resumed on October 5, heralded the afternoon before by Indian dances in a public square near the White House. Sioux "jumped, yelled, and whooped upon the green" to the amusement of thousands of Washingtonians who filled the streets and hung from buildings

[13] *Daily National Intelligencer* (Washington), September 29 and 30, October 2 and 4, 1837.

[14] Joshua Pilcher to William Clark, September 5, 1837, and to C. A. Harris, October 20, 1837, LR, OIA, RG 75, NA; C. A. Harris to Joshua Pilcher, October 27, 1837, LS, OIA, RG 75, NA.

for a better view of the scantly clad, painted performers. The Sac and Foxes of the Mississippi, led by the renowned chiefs Black Hawk and Keokuk and escorted by General Joseph Street, had intended to dance in the square, but when the crowd disobeyed police directions and grew disorderly, they refused to dance.

On Saturday, October 7, General Street and Joshua led all the Sac and Foxes and Ioways to the church. Vice-President Johnson and other administration leaders gathered there with the delegations to hear speeches by Commissioner Harris, Keokuk, and several Ioway chiefs. After the speeches the meeting adjourned until Monday morning, when treaty negotiations resumed before a large audience. By mid-week public interest in the council had "very considerably abated." A colorful delegation of Winnebagos had arrived in town, replacing Black Hawk and Keokuk as lions of the day.[15] Behind closed doors in the Indian Office negotiators had been ironing out the details of treaties between the government and the Yankton Sioux and the Sac and Foxes. When the documents were signed, another public session was held in the church on Saturday morning, October 21, to celebrate the event. Seventy-four Indians, two cabinet members, several Indian agents, including Joshua, and other distinguished observers packed the platform to watch Secretary of War Poinsett present the Indians "handsome silver medals" engraved on one side, with the likeness of President Van Buren, and on the other, "a tomahawk reversed and crossed with a pipe . . . [of] Peace and Friendship." Two Indians, in return, gave Poinsett a calumet and pledged peace with the Whites "forever." Then, with handshaking all around, the council broke up.[16]

That same day, October 21, Commissioner Harris ordered

[15] *Daily National Intelligencer* (Washington), October 6, 7, 9, 10, and 16, 1837.

[16] *Ibid.*, October 23, 1837. For the text of the Yankton Sioux and Sac and Fox treaties see Peters (ed.), *Statutes at Large*, VII, 540–44.

Joshua to take his delegation to Philadelphia, New York City, and Boston before returning to the West, and empowered him to draw up to $6,000 to cover expenses. The administration wished to impress the Indians with the skill and ingenuity of the American people by showing them factories, navy yards, and fortifications. Joshua was told to escort the Indians to places of public amusement and to be seen by as many people as possible. He was authorized to return to Washington with the Indians for a brief visit before heading west, but he preferred to remain in or near the capital as much as possible, for political reasons, and was not particularly pleased to escort the Indians on the full Washington to Boston circuit.[17] Nevertheless, on Sunday, October 22, he and his delegation, with all the other Indians except the Winnebagos, boarded the Washington branch of the Baltimore and Ohio Railroad and began the tour via Baltimore and Philadelphia to New York City.[18] In Philadelphia the Indians went to Cookes' Equestrian Circus and were "much pleased" by the performance and particularly "engaged" by a large gas chandelier illuminating the building.[19] In New York City, Joshua and his assistants, Major Chauncey Bush and Nathan Rice, shared the duty of escorting the Indians, by rented omnibus, to the theater; to the fair at Niblo's Garden, where American-made objects were displayed; and to the Stuyvesant Institute to hear George Catlin, the eminent painter, lecture on his Indian portraits and exhibit tribal artifacts to "multitudes of [gentlemen and] delicate women" who jammed the "ferociously, cruelly hot" room. When Catlin showed them a portrait of a Sioux chief, a hush fell over the Indians, and then a strange whisper—she-e-e-e—ran through the ranks of the Sioux. Catlin explained to the others in the audience that Joshua had just

[17] C. A. Harris to Joshua Pilcher, October 21, 1837, and to Major C. Bush, October 21, 1837, LS, OIA, RG 75, NA.

[18] *Daily National Intelligencer* (Washington), October 24, 1837; *Sun* (Baltimore), October 24, 1837.

[19] *National Gazette and Literary Register* (Philadelphia), October 26, 1837.

told him that the Indians murmured because the chief in the painting had died in battle with a buffalo bull after he had learned of his son's death and had vowed to kill the first man or animal he met.[20]

When the delegations reached Boston, by steamboat from New York City, on October 27, Joshua immediately turned over responsibility for the Sioux, Sac and Foxes, and Ioways to Nathan Rice and went south, to care for a Sioux chief left in Baltimore "at the point of death," in the hands of an old Sac interpreter and an Indian Office employee. Joshua explained to Commissioner Harris that the Sioux with him in Boston had asked that he return to Baltimore to care for their friend and that he, in his order of October 21, had given him permission to leave the delegation in charge of an assistant if circumstances demanded it. Joshua reached Philadelphia on the night of October 31, where the Sac interpreter met him to report that the Sioux chief had died in Baltimore.[21] Joshua, now free to pay a brief visit to Washington, became ill, and had to cancel his trip to the capital, but recovered in time to welcome his Indian delegation back to Philadelphia from their grand tour of the Northeast and start west with them.[22]

They retraced their route across Pennsylvania by canalboat and

[20] *Evening Post* (New York City), October 25 and 26, 1837; *New-York Spectator*, October 26 and 30, 1837; *Morning Courier and New-York Enquirer*, October 25, 1837; *Morning Herald* (New York City), October 25 and 26, 1837; *Daily National Intelligencer* (Washington), October 25, 1837; *Daily Evening Transcript* (Boston), October 30, 1837, quoting a New York City newspaper.

[21] *New York Journal of Commerce*, October 27, 1837; *Daily Evening Transcript* (Boston), October 27, 1837; *Boston Morning Post*, October 28, 1837; Joshua Pilcher to C. A. Harris, October 27, 1837, and to Nathan Rice, October 27, 1837; and C. Bush to C. A. Harris, October 24, 1837, LR, OIA, RG 75, NA.

[22] Joshua Pilcher to C. A. Harris, November 1 and 4, 1837, LR, OIA, RG 75, NA. For information on the Indians in Boston and in New York City between October 27 and November 3 see the *Daily Evening Transcript* (Boston), October 28, 30, and 31, 1837; the Boston *Atlas*, October 31, 1837 quoted in the *Daily National Intelligencer* (Washington), November 7, 1837; the *Evening Post* (New York City), October 31 and November 1, 1837; the *New-York Daily*

Interior of the trading post at Bellevue, 1852.
From a drawing by Heinrich B. Möllhausen.

Sir George Simpson
From a mezzotint by S. Pearce

Stephen F. Austin

Thomas Hart Benton in 1817
From a painting by
Sarah Miriam Peale

Pierre Chouteau, Jr.

assistance of John Haverty, Joseph A. Sire, of the American Fur Company, and one member of the Riddick family, he probably would have failed to meet his disbursing obligations in 1839 on the upper Mississippi. Before he hired Haverty as clerk, he had sent him to Prairie du Chien with $95,000 in specie assigned to John Fleming, Jr., the United States Indian claims commissioner there. Sire and Riddick helped Haverty make the transfer of specie to Fleming without incident, and Haverty returned to St. Louis in October, 1839. Joshua was grateful and named Haverty his clerk in the new year.[22]

In addition to the time that Joshua had to give to disbursing funds, receiving visitors at the office, issuing trading licenses for the Indian country, and account-keeping, he also gave many hours to work on the details of supply contracts between contractors and the Indian Office.[23] The American Fur Company, through astute politicking in Washington, was usually awarded most of the annual contracts to supply the annuity goods in the St. Louis superintendency. They also stocked a great variety of Indian goods in their St. Louis warehouse, and Joshua was in almost constant contact with Chouteau and his representatives. He was accused of being prejudiced in favor of the company because he had worked for them at Council Bluffs and had co-existed peacefully with them on the upper Missouri most of the time he had been sub-agent and agent to the Sioux. Joshua was not a company tool, however. No man's pawn, not even Chouteau's, he knew that the American

1839, and E. A. Hitchcock to T. H. Crawford, June 7, 1839, LR, OIA, RG 75, NA; T. H. Crawford to Joshua Pilcher, June 15, 1839, LS, OIA, RG 75, NA; Joshua Pilcher to Pierre Chouteau, Jr., May 16, 1839, Chouteau MSS, MoSHi.

[22] Joshua Pilcher to John Haverty, July 25, 1839, and to T. H. Crawford, October 28, 1839, LR, OIA, RG 75, NA; Joshua Pilcher to John Haverty, August 14, 1839, Indian Trade and Fur Companies Envelope, MoSHi; Lawrence Taliaferro to Joshua Pilcher, September 2, 1839, Taliaferro LB, Vol. 5, pp. 201–202, MnHi.

[23] For detailed information on the Indian trading licenses that Joshua granted between 1839 and 1841 see the License Abstracts in LR, OIA, RG 75, NA.

Fur Company virtually controlled steamboat transportation on the upper Missouri and possessed the most reliable means of carrying annuities to the upriver tribes. He also knew, from experience, that their merchandise was good, frequently superior to goods available from other suppliers. Aware that Chouteau's voice was much stronger than his in Washington, he knew, ever so well that he could lose his job if he opposed the company vigorously. Thus, he co-operated with Chouteau up to a point, and the company co-operated with him. Rather than endanger his career by fighting over annuity and supply contracts, he worked quietly to guarantee that goods sent the Indians were of satisfactory quality, and he carefully investigated shipments to make sure that the Indians received goods they really needed.[24]

In spite of his waspish temper, Joshua was an able politician who knew how to humor the American Fur Company, a vested interest, without losing his integrity, and realized he could not be a lukewarm Democrat if he expected to hold his job for long. The panic of 1837 had hurt the Van Buren administration, and the Whigs who were attacking Jackson's heirs from all sides might turn them out of the White House in 1840. The Democratic party called, and Joshua loyally answered the call. About the time he went to work to help shore up the party in Missouri, late in the spring of 1839, Dougherty called on Joshua in St. Louis and requested leave to visit Washington. When told to apply in writing, he disregarded the suggestion and left immediately for the capital, as Joshua reported to Crawford, to promote "his own personal views." Dougherty was angry that Joshua had won the superin-

[24] Joshua Pilcher to T. H. Crawford, December 26, 1839 (two letters), February 8, September 1, and December 30, 1840, and March 17, 1841, LR, OIA, RG 75, NA; Joshua Pilcher's Property Returns, Clark MSS, Vol. 19, KHi; American Fur Company Ledgers BB, CC, DD, and EE, MoSHi, all contain Pilcher merchandise accounts for annuities, presents to Indians visiting St. Louis, office supplies, and personal items.

tendency and Joshua knew it, but he said he held only "personal good feeling" for Dougherty. A short time later Dougherty resigned as Indian agent and in 1840 won a seat, as a Whig, in the Missouri Legislature. He campaigned for Harrison against Van Buren that year, defeated an attempt by the American Fur Company to incorporate in Missouri, and urged the Indian Office to move the St. Louis superintendency to Clay County in western Missouri—there was a powerful anti-Chouteau, anti-Benton clique at the county seat, Liberty—or even, across the river out of the state, to Fort Leavenworth.[25]

During 1839 and 1840 Joshua participated in Democratic party meetings and committee work in St. Louis, especially in Benton's behalf.[26] He fought the Whig "Liberty Birds" who "feathered their nest" with fat government contracts and strongly opposed the plan of the Dougherty-Whig-Liberty faction to move his office from St. Louis to some "miserable, dirty frontier village, with a *suitable* incumbent, who loved *his* interest and *theirs*, more than an honest & impartial discharge of his duties."[27] In December, 1840, when he heard that delegates to the Missouri Legislature from Clay County, planned to "memorialize Congress to establish [a superintendency] at Liberty or Fort Leavenworth," he wrote to Benton's good friend, Democratic Lieutenant Governor–elect Meredith M. Marmaduke of Missouri. In a five-page letter he explained why the superintendency should remain at St. Louis; told the Lieutenant Governor that since 1835 the Congress had received and ignored four similar memorials; explained to Marmaduke the complex duties of the St. Louis superintendent of

[25] Joshua Pilcher to T. H. Crawford, June 12, 1839, LR, OIA, RG 75, NA; John Dougherty to James H. Birch, March 15, 1841, Dougherty Papers, MoSHi; Stauf, "Dougherty," *Mid-America*, Vol. XVI (January, 1934), 144.

[26] *Missouri Argus* (St. Louis), July 31, 1839, and June 24, 1840.

[27] Joshua Pilcher to A. L. Davis, August 14, 1839, Clark MSS, Vol. 7, p. 28, KHi; Joshua Pilcher to T. H. Crawford, May 20, 1839, LR, OIA, RG 75, NA.

Indian affairs; and emphasized how difficult it would be to run his office from a tiny community "in the interior of Clay County."[28] The Lieutenant Governor agreed completely with Joshua's point of view and replied within three days to thank him for his long report. Joshua returned the courtesy in a short Christmas Eve letter to Marmaduke: "I can say; and with pride too; that I killed [the proposal to move the superintendency] three times before I ever had a thought of filling the office; and I feel verry [sic] confident . . . that I shall defeat it again in Congress." Suffice to say, the office remained in St. Louis.[29]

Joshua viewed with mixed emotions the Indian agents and sub-agents reporting to him. He was cordial to Dougherty's successor, Joseph V. Hamilton, and, when Hamilton took up his duties at Bellevue, he thanked Joshua "for the patience with which you initiated me in the duties of my office" and criticized Dougherty for the poor condition of the post. In July, 1839, Joshua had recommended to Commissioner Crawford that the Indian Office allot $150 to $400 to repair the agency buildings at Bellevue rather than spend $3,500 to build a new agency near the mouth of the Platte River. Dougherty had favored the larger expenditure, but Crawford agreed with Joshua and authorized $200 for repairs of the old post. Hamilton and several other men carefully examined the condition of the buildings at the agency and reported that the $200 would be wasted in repairs. They needed ten times that much to erect entirely new buildings. Unabashed, Joshua wrote Crawford for more money, and, once again, Crawford responded favorably and provided $1,500 for new buildings.[30]

---

28 Joshua Pilcher to M. M. Marmaduke, December 16, 1840, pp. 1–4, Marmaduke Papers, MoHi, and p. 5, Sappington Family Papers, MoSHi.

29 Joshua Pilcher to M. M. Marmaduke, December 24, 1840, Sappington Family Papers, MoSHi.

30 Joseph V. Hamilton to Joshua Pilcher, August 15, 1839, and Joshua Pilcher to T. H. Crawford, July 6, 1839, and January 1, 1840, LR, OIA, RG 75, NA; T. H. Crawford to Joshua Pilcher, July 25, 1839, LS, OIA, RG 75, NA;

Joshua also appreciated Anthony L. Davis and told Crawford that Davis, the Osage River sub-agent, was "generally a very correct and attentive officer."[31] No Upper Missouri Agent to the Sioux, Cheyennes, and Poncas was appointed while Joshua was in office, and the Great Nemaha sub-agency, for the Ioways and Sac and Foxes of the Missouri, was without an agent most of the time between 1839 and 1841. He respected Richard W. Cummins, the Fort Leavenworth agent and, in contrast, despised Stephen Cooper, the Council Bluffs sub-agent to the Potawatomis.[32] Cooper was bothered with whiskey traders who preyed upon the Indians in his jurisdiction. His job was difficult, to be sure, but he did not keep accurate accounts, sent in exaggerated reports, and exceeded his authority by granting trading licenses that Joshua revoked immediately. Joshua twice reported Cooper to the Indian Office and advised Crawford to transfer the Indians under Cooper to another agent. Crawford delayed action, however, until Joshua wrote a third letter, on April 28, 1841, begging the Indian Office to remove Cooper, charging, "he is not only *incompetent* but *incapable* of being made otherwise." This time Crawford acted and replaced Cooper with James W. Deaderick.[33]

Near the end of his first nine months in office, Joshua, for the first time, dared leave his clerk in charge of the St. Louis office while he went to Washington to settle his complicated quarterly accounts. Crawford at first denied Joshua leave, but then changed his mind and "cheerfully granted" sixty days. Joshua left St.

Joshua Pilcher to J. V. Hamilton, September 15, 1840, Clark MSS, Vol. 7, p. 85, KHi.

[31] Joshua Pilcher to T. H. Crawford, October 16, 1839, LR, OIA, RG 75, NA.

[32] *Ibid.*, November 4, 1840, *ibid.*

[33] *Ibid.*, November 4 and 21, 1840, and April 28, 1841, and to Stephen Cooper, March 16 and July 21, 1840, and Albert M. Lea to T. H. Crawford, August 31, 1841, *ibid.*

Louis on January 12, 1840, for the East.[34] In the capital he conferred with Sanford, of the American Fur Company, about Indian merchandise; arranged his accounts with the second auditor; and was instructed, by Crawford, early in February, to investigate Glasgow, Harrison and Company (James Glasgow and James Harrison), traders and importers of Howard County, Missouri, and points south-southwest, who had contracted with the government to supply $500,000 in food to the Indians.[35] On February 18, Joshua left Washington, probably by stage, for Louisville, where he boarded a steamboat for Cairo. There, he transferred to another boat for St. Louis and, by chance, met aboard a man from Howard County who gave him information on the case under investigation.

Joshua reached St. Louis late in February. He worked in the office a few days, then, on March 6, caught a steamboat up the Missouri River to Arrow Rock and took a room a few miles away, in a tavern at Glasgow, in Howard County. He spent a week in the area investigating Glasgow and Harrison. He heard that they were in Arkansas, but learned little about the contracts they had made with the government. On March 13 he returned to St. Louis on the *Rhine*, worked in the office a week, and then booked passage on the *Maid of Orleans* for Arkansas. At Montgomery's Point, a squalid, lawless village near the mouth of the White River, he transferred to a boat headed up the Arkansas River to Little Rock. There, he checked into the Western Exchange Hotel and learned that Glasgow and Harrison had left Little Rock for Washington and that A. J. Raines, who had written Crawford in 1839 about the Glasgow and Harrison contracts, was also out of

---

[34] T. H. Crawford to Joshua Pilcher, November 20, and December 16, 1839, LS, OIA, RG 75, NA; Joshua Pilcher to Mr. Palmer, January 16, 1840, Chouteau MSS, MoSHi.

[35] Ramsay Crooks to Pierre Chouteau, Jr., No. 7487, January 28, 1840, American Fur Company Papers, NHi; Joshua Pilcher to T. H. Crawford, May 5, 1840, LR, OIA, RG 75, NA.

town. However, Captain Richard D'Cantillon Collins, the government disbursing agent who had made the contracts with Glasgow, Harrison and Company, was in town. He met Joshua at the hotel and promised to make all his records available to him as soon as his clerk returned from Arkansas Post. Joshua waited two days, until March 29, when Collins called upon him again; discussed his accounts, but did not produce them for Joshua's examination because his clerk still was absent; and promised to give Joshua within a few days a written statement that no government money remained in his hands.

While Collins stalled, Joshua took the *Lady Morgan* up the Arkansas River to Fort Smith in search of Raines, the informant, but he was nowhere to be seen. Joshua learned from an officer at Fort Gibson that Raines refused—rumor held he was probably bribed—to press charges against Glasgow and Harrison. Joshua returned to Little Rock on April 14 and struggled with Collins for nearly a week before the disbursing agent gave him abstracts of his accounts. Collins indicated that he was prepared to go to court to defend his name if the Indian Office charged him formally with taking a cut (one-sixth, Crawford speculated) on the contracts he had given Glasgow and Harrison. Since Joshua knew that he could learn nothing more in Little Rock, he left for St. Louis and reached home a week later. On May 5 he sent Crawford a formal report on the investigation and concluded reluctantly that "there appears nothing in the transactions to justify the belief that [Collins] had an interest in either of the contracts." The following February, however, Collins was "dismissed from the services" for "having failed to render his accounts for monies advanced to him."[36]

[36] T. H. Crawford to Joshua Pilcher, December 31, 1839, and February 8, 1840, LS, OIA, RG 75, NA; Joshua Pilcher to T. H. Crawford, April 30 and May 5, 1840, LR, OIA, RG 75, NA; Files 6317–A and B, RICC, RG 279, NA; Joel R. Poinsett to President Van Buren, February 24, 1841, and General Order No. 13, February 26, 1841, Records of the Adjutant General's Office, RG 94, NA.

Joshua settled down in St. Louis for the summer of 1840 following his tiring, frustrating trips to western Missouri and the Arkansas country. Haverty ran the office smoothly and, although Joshua still needed to work long hours, he understood his complex duties as superintendent better than he had the previous summer. He complained that the Indian Office did not warn him when Indian refugees, evicted in the East under the government's Indian removal policy, were due to pass through on their way to new homes in the West. Since he had to provide them food, clothing, shelter, and emergency transportation, he wanted to know when they were scheduled to enter his jurisdiction. The Indian Office, in turn, complained that he did not support zealously the Choctaw Academy in Kentucky by sending Indian students to the institution. Joshua in return protested to Crawford: He had sent four boys to the school in the spring, but he refused to use force to recruit other students. The Indians had heard bad reports about the academy—apparently, some of the reports were true—and most of the Indians were unwilling to send their sons to Kentucky, where one boy had died. Joshua had become more and more suspicious of the academy because it was shakily financed and run by political hacks under Vice-President Johnson's patronage.[37] In contrast, he held in high esteem the Roman Catholic mission school for the Kickapoos in Kansas and recommended to Crawford that the government double the amount of money allotted the mission.[38]

[37] Joshua Pilcher to T. H. Crawford, October 13, 1840, LR, OIA, RG 75, NA; T. H. Crawford to Joshua Pilcher, June 27, 1840, and March 17, 1841, LS, OIA, RG 75, NA. For a short history of The Choctaw Academy, see Mrs. Shelley D. Rouse, "Colonel Dick Johnson's Choctaw Academy: A Forgotten Educational Experiment," *Ohio Archaeological and Historical Publications*, Vol. XXV (1916), 88–117.

[38] Joshua Pilcher to T. H. Crawford, August 19, 1839, LR, OIA, RG 75, NA; Gilbert J. Garraghan, *The Jesuits of the Middle United States*, I, 415–18, and II, 199.

In June, two months after Joshua returned to St. Louis from Little Rock, he received a visitor with a serious problem at the office. John Beach, Indian agent to the Sac and Foxes of the Mississippi, asked Joshua to visit his agency in Iowa, to deliver personally the cash annuity for 1840 due the Sac and Foxes of the Mississippi. Beach said he was inexperienced in making an annuity payment; he had just taken over the agency from his father-in-law, General Joseph M. Street, who had died in May; he wanted to learn from Joshua the proper procedure to follow; he had heard complaints about earlier annuity payments; and he believed that Joshua, who was disbursing agent for Iowa, could silence the rumors by distributing the money in person. Joshua, not anxious to go to Iowa, wrote for advice. He noted to Crawford that Beach was the second person who had suggested that he personally make the Sac and Fox annuity payment. In mid-August the Commissioner advised Joshua to use his discretion—go to Iowa if he wished. Joshua thought it over for a few days and decided to make the trip. He had planned to go up the Missouri River early in the fall to distribute annuities to Indians in his own superintendency, but now he changed his plans and sent Haverty upriver on September 13 with annuities for the Great Nemaha Agency, where Congreve Jackson, appointed sub-agent in 1839, had never reported for duty, and for the Council Bluffs Sub-Agency, where Cooper was incapable of distributing a large annuity correctly.[39]

Joshua filled a box with bank notes, hired a fast two-horse carriage and a dependable driver, and set out on September 16 for Beach's agency in the Des Moines River Valley of southeastern Iowa.[40] When he reached the agency a few days later, he found the Sac and Foxes divided into two factions: one group of "inde-

---

[39] Joshua Pilcher to T. H. Crawford, July 1 and October 7, 1840, LR, OIA, RG 75, NA; T. H. Crawford to Joshua Pilcher, August 14, 1840, LS, OIA, RG 75, NA.
[40] File 6317–B, RICC, RG 279, NA.

pendents . . . wanted the money distributed on principles of justice and equity among the different bands and to the heads of families"; the other group, led by Keokuk, wanted the annuity given out "to a few of the chiefs, to be distributed by them alone."[41] Beach had sent for troops to maintain order and had notified Robert Lucas, governor of Iowa Territory, that Joshua was coming to the agency. Lucas arrived nine days later, on September 27, and sensed that the Indians were "in sullen mood": after conferring with Joshua and Beach the following morning, he assembled the Indians in council, but after many long speeches the council failed and broke up. Joshua had expected to pay the Indians as soon as he reached the agency, but in deference to Lucas and Beach, he had delayed payment until the council could settle Indian differences amicably. Keokuk, "apprehend[ing] some danger if the money was not taken away," sent Joshua a message, after the meeting, advising him to pack up the bank notes and leave the agency. A few hours later, early on the twenty-ninth, Joshua again met with Lucas and Beach and decided to take Keokuk's advice. Beach said the Indians wanted specie, not paper money, and Joshua agreed to take the bank notes back to St. Louis, convert them to specie, and forward the specie to the agency whenever the Indians settled their quarrel. One group of Indians told Lucas that they intended to seize the money, but he quieted them, and Joshua returned peacefully to St. Louis, by October 3, with the annuity.[42]

At the end of the month Governor Lucas sent the Indian Office a long report on the Sac and Foxes. He accused the American Fur Company of deceit and said that company traders had used

[41] Message from Governor Robert Lucas to the Council and House of Representatives of Iowa Territory, November 3, 1840, reprinted in Benjamin F. Shambaugh (ed.), *Executive Journal of Iowa 1838–1843*, 257.

[42] Joshua Pilcher to T. H. Crawford, October 5 and 7, 1840, LR, OIA, RG 75, NA; Shambaugh (ed.), *Executive Journal*, 257–59; "Indian Affairs of Iowa in 1840," *Annals of Iowa*, Vol. XV (April, 1926), 265–71.

Keokuk and Beach to break up the Indian council at the Iowa agency. He declared that the specie question was not important in the negotiations: the real issue was the threat, to the company's control of trade and to Keokuk's control of the Sac and Foxes, posed by the independent Indian faction who wanted the annuity distributed equally to all chiefs. According to the Governor, the faction led by Keokuk wanted to distribute the money to the few pro-company chiefs who co-operated with the trading monopoly. In St. Louis, Joshua converted the $42,000 worth of bank notes into specie and informed Beach, by letter, in November, that the money was ready to distribute whenever he called for it. Joshua also made it clear that it would be neither "convenient or agreeable" for him to visit the Iowa agency again that fall. He had made two fruitless trips into the field in seven months, one to Arkansas and one to Iowa, and he did not intend to become embroiled in the Sac and Fox controversy. Lucas ordered Beach to obtain the annuity and to distribute it to approximately thirty Indians representing both factions, but Beach refused to ask Joshua for the money before the following spring. Eventually, the annuity payment issue was resolved by compromise, and Keokuk won control of the Sac and Foxes.[43]

During the month of October, 1840, following his return to St. Louis from Iowa, Joshua was far more interested in the heated presidential contest between Van Buren and Harrison than he was in the Sac and Fox annuity question. He worked for the Democratic ticket, particularly for the hard-money faction of the party in Missouri, against heavy opposition from the Whigs in St. Louis. Mistakenly anticipating victory for Van Buren, he declared (a newspaper reported) that he would not hold office under a Har-

---

[43] Joshua Pilcher to John Beach, November 17 and December 31, 1840, and John Beach to Joshua Pilcher, March 31, 1841, LR, OIA, RG 75, NA; Shambaugh (ed.), *Executive Journal*, 258–59; "Indian Affairs . . . 1840," *Annals of Iowa*, Vol. XV (April, 1926), 270–71.

rison administration and, in event of a Whig triumph, would resign as superintendent of Indian affairs and work for Benton for President in 1844.[44] When Harrison lost Missouri by approximately 7,000 votes (fewer than Benton, who campaigned across the state for Van Buren, expected), but beat Van Buren nationally, the *Missouri Republican* called Joshua "a fit subject for the pruning hook." Other newspapers such as the *Louisville Journal* joined the Whig clamor for Joshua's removal, while the Democratic *St. Louis Argus* grew "most painfully solicitous for his retention in office."[45] One of the many applicants for Joshua's job charged, in a letter to John Bell, the new secretary of war, that Joshua had bet $500 on the presidential contest and lost. If Joshua placed an election bet, he probably wagered far less than $500, but the story of the bet, together with the report of his declaration that he would not serve under Harrison, gave the Whigs ammunition to snipe at him in the months following Harrison's victory. He was a partisan Democrat, they said, and deserved to be fired.[46]

A few days after the election Joshua applied to Crawford for leave to attend to private business in Philadelphia and Washington, but added, in his letter of application, that "other important reasons" made the trip necessary as well. The reasons were obvious; likely to be removed from office when Harrison was inaugurated in March, 1841, he intended to spend the winter in Washington fighting for his job. Crawford granted him leave two weeks after he applied, and on January 1 he set out for the the capital.[47] Washington buzzed with political speculation that winter: What would a Whig administration be like and how

[44] *Daily Missouri Republican* (St. Louis), April 12, 1841.

[45] The *Louisville Journal* quoted in *ibid.*

[46] Thomas C. Hindman to Secretary of War John Bell, May 13, 1841, LR, OIA, RG 75, NA.

[47] Joshua Pilcher to T. H. Crawford, November 10, 1840, *ibid.*; T. H. Crawford to Joshua Pilcher, November 24, 1840, LS, OIA, RG 75, NA; John Haverty to C. Jackson, January 21, 1841, Clark MSS, Vol. 7, p. 114, KHi.

many Democrats would be kicked out of office? Joshua settled down in the capital for three months, went over his accounts with the second auditor, and talked to politicians who could help him stay in office. In the midst of these activities he still took his responsibilities as superintendent seriously enough to protest to Crawford when a missionary turned up in town leading an unauthorized Potawatomi Indian delegation from the Indian country, and he advised the Commissioner to speed efforts to acquire title to lands still held by Indians in Iowa.[48]

In February, Chouteau wrote the Indian Office in support of Joshua, and one of Joshua's friends asked Senator John J. Crittenden of Kentucky to use his influence to keep Joshua in office—"he is a gentleman an *honest man* and *more capable* than any man in the government."[49] Otherwise few letters of application for Joshua's job or letters supporting him reached Washington before March 4, inaugural day. The letter writers waited for Harrison to take office. Apparently the new administration had not yet selected anyone to fill Joshua's position, and when Harrison died suddenly, in early April, the Tyler administration was too busy with other problems to name a superintendent of Indian affairs at St. Louis immediately.

Joshua stayed in Washington until after Harrison died. Early in April, he returned to duty in St. Louis, and awaited the Whig verdict on his job.[50]

---

[48] Joshua Pilcher to T. H. Crawford, February 15, and March 10, 1841, LR, OIA, RG 75, NA. Crawford instructed Joshua, on March 1, 1841, "to embrace the most fitting opportunities to hold treaties with these [Iowa] tribes for such a removal, and for the cession of their remaining lands in Iowa Territory." Then, three weeks later, Crawford suspended his order. See T. H. Crawford to Joshua Pilcher, March 1 and 25, 1841, LS, OIA, RG 75, NA.

[49] Pierre Chouteau, Jr., to T. H. Crawford, February 22, 1841, and J. Samuel to J. J. Crittenden, February 9, 1841, LR, OIA, RG 75, NA.

[50] Joshua Pilcher to T. H. Crawford, April 5, 1841, *ibid.*; T. H. Crawford to Joshua Pilcher, March 30, 1841, LS, OIA, RG 75, NA.

AFTER HARRISON'S INAUGURATION several men applied, or were recommended, for the job of superintendent of Indian affairs at St. Louis. Some of the candidates disliked Joshua and told the Indian Office why: William N. Wickliffe claimed that Joshua caused the Van Buren administration to remove him as disbursing agent for the St. Louis district in favor of Ethan A. Hitchcock, and Thomas C. Hindman accused Joshua of "improper interference in Elections, on the side of the last administration."[1] But Dougherty, the leading candidate, recommended by several prominent businessmen and politicians, did not explain his feelings about Joshua to the Indian Office. He was a loyal Whig, and his opinions on Joshua and the American Fur Company were well known in Washington and the West. In a letter to James H. Birch of Liberty he summed up the battle that he faced with Joshua and the company: "Pilcher is a first rate Bentonian wire worker and if reports be true the American Fur Company are quite as much interested in his retention . . . as he is himself." In addition he predicted, accurately: "They will leave no stone unturned to keep him in office, and . . . they will be quite as active in their exertion to keep me out."[2]

Chouteau had opened the company campaign to retain Joshua and to defeat Dougherty in his February letter to the Indian Office. Now Ramsay Crooks, his associate in New York City, suggested that the company approach the Wisconsin delegation in

[1] R. Wickliffe, Jr., to the Office of Indian Affairs, March 8, 1841, and Thomas C. Hindman to Secretary of War Bell, May 13 and 20, 1841, LR, OIA, RG 75, NA.

[2] John Dougherty to James H. Birch, March 15, 1841, Dougherty Papers, MoSHi.

Congress to pressure Secretary of War Bell to support Joshua. *"Pilcher must not be displaced,"* Crooks wrote Chouteau on March 12, "he is too important a man to lose, and no effort must be spared to save him."[3] And so the battle lines were drawn in March and April between Joshua's friends, who worked feverishly to keep him in office, and the partisan supporters of other candidates, particularly of Dougherty, who were just as determined to capture the position. Then, on April 20, James H. Birch, Thornton Grimsley, and a few other Missouri Whigs recommended another candidate—a compromise candidate?—Charles Keemle of St. Louis, Joshua's former lieutenant in the fur trade, one of those who had survived the Jones-Immell massacre. Secretary of War Bell and Commissioner Crawford jumped at the opportunity to support a compromise candidate and appointed Keemle on May 25 while the Senate was in recess.[4]

Crawford ordered Joshua to turn over to Keemle the funds, records, and property of the office as soon as the new superintendent was ready to take office.[5] Between June 3 and 5 the St. Louis newspapers announced Keemle's appointment with varying degrees of enthusiasm. The Democratic *Missouri Argus* admitted that Keemle was capable, but blasted the administration for stretching Joshua "upon the Political Guillotine" for political activity in favor of Van Buren. The newspaper swore, inaccurately, that Joshua had "never been known to make stump speeches, write for public papers, take an active part at public meetings, or to electioneer at the polls." The editor characterized him, instead, as "an open, bold, decided Western Man who is above concealment of his opinion" (the last five words were certainly accurate), and

---

[3] Ramsay Crooks to Pierre Chouteau, Jr., March 12, 1841, Chouteau MSS, MoSHi.

[4] James H. Birch, Thornton Grimsley et al to the Office of Indian Affairs, April 20, 1841, LR, OIA, RG 75, NA; T. H. Crawford to Charles Keemle, May 25, 1841, LS, OIA, RG 75, NA; *Journal of the Senate*, V, 390.

[5] T. H. Crawford to Joshua Pilcher, May 24, 1841, LS, OIA, RG 75, NA.

asked why it was wrong for Joshua to express his political opinions but right for Keemle to be "a thousand times more active in politics."[6] The answer was obvious, and the *Daily Missouri Republican* gave it to the *Argus* on June 7: Keemle was a private citizen and held no office in the fall of 1840 "to bring into conflict with the freedom of elections." The *Republican* applauded the new superintendent because he opposed Benton and refused to do the Senator's "dirty work," and threatened to publish "the facts of the proscription exercised when [Joshua] got the office [of superintendent] in 1839."[7]

The *St. Louis New Era* predicted that Keemle would clean up the "enormous quantity of dirty work in the deportment of our Indian Affairs" and called for general reform in government. The *Daily Evening Gazette* and the *Daily Pennant and Native American*, however, were more temperate than the other three newspapers in their editorial comment on Keemle's appointment. The *Pennant* presumed that the Whigs were satisfied by the appointment, while the *Gazette* complimented Joshua for doing "his duty faithfully" and reminded the public that he was simply a victim of the spoils system and that when the Democrats returned to power they would fire his successor.[8] Meanwhile, Joshua put Haverty in charge of the office; closed his disbursements through June 10; and, the following morning, left by stage for Washington to settle his accounts with the government.[9]

Five days before Joshua left St. Louis, Keemle told the *Republican* that poor health—his physician had ordered him to go south for the winter—forced him to decline the superintendency.[10] On

[6] *Missouri Argus* (St. Louis), June 4, 1841.

[7] *Daily Missouri Republican* (St. Louis), June 4, and 7, 1841.

[8] *St. Louis New Era*, June 4, 1841; *Daily Evening Gazette* (St. Louis), June 4, 1841; *Daily Pennant and Native American* (St. Louis), June 5, 1841.

[9] John Haverty to R. W. Cummins, June 16, 1841, and to John Beach, June 19, 1841, Clark MSS, Vol. 7, pp. 131–32, KHi.

[10] *Daily Missouri Republican* (St. Louis), June 7, 1841.

June 10, the very day Joshua closed disbursements, Keemle formally declined the office in a letter to the Secretary of War, thereby reopening the conflict over the position.[11] Joshua knew, before leaving St. Louis, that Keemle had declined to serve—the story was in the newspapers, and everyone talked about it—and he probably went east as much to seek reinstatement as to settle his accounts. He reached Washington on June 21, took a room at the Columbian Hotel, and waited—but not long.[12] The administration, caught without a substitute for Keemle, notified Joshua, on June 23, that he was still superintendent.[13] The *St. Louis New Era* reported, just before Joshua reached Washington, that a movement was under way to restore him to office led by "an association of wealthy persons, having trading posts amongst all the important tribes of Indians of the West."[14] The story was correct; Crooks and Chouteau were lobbying vigorously to keep Joshua in office. Nonetheless, the administration refused to restore him and agreed only to retain him until a new man took office. Dougherty, however, was not to be that new man. Although his friends recommended him to the Indian Office once again, Chouteau excluded him from candidacy. On July 11, Crooks wrote Chouteau that he thought that Secretary of War Bell "will not give the place to any one likely to annoy you."[15]

On July 22, President Tyler withdrew Keemle's appointment and nominated David Dawson Mitchell to be superintendent of Indian affairs at St. Louis.[16] Mitchell, born in Louisa County,

[11] *St. Louis New Era*, June 11, 1841.

[12] File 8143, RICC, RG 279, NA.

[13] T. H. Crawford to Joshua Pilcher, June 23, 1841, LS, OIA, RG 75, NA.

[14] *St. Louis New Era*, June 18, 1841.

[15] Ramsay Crooks to Pierre Chouteau, Jr., June 23 and 27 and July 11, 1841, Chouteau MSS, MoSHi; Recommendations for John Dougherty from John Wilson, S. C. Owens, Martin Thomas, and Silas Reed, July 10–14, 1841, Registers of Letters Received by the Secretary of War, RG 107, NA.

[16] *Journal of the Senate*, V, 409.

Virginia, just south of Joshua's childhood home in Culpeper, was an American Fur Company employee, but hardly a company man. Crooks reminded Chouteau, nearly a month before Tyler nominated Mitchell, that Mitchell's "conduct . . . does not give him any claims to your good offices," yet admitted that "with all his sins he will answer better than anyone that has thus far put in his name for the appointment."[17] Joshua remained in Washington through the summer, prolonging his stay from week to week, while he settled his accounts and used his influence to weed out undesirable candidates, especially those who belonged to the Whig faction from Liberty, Missouri, who applied for his office. He was amused by the rush for position in the Tyler administration and enjoyed the "very animated and interesting senate debates before crowded galleries." In fact, he accepted his forced retirement rather philosophically. In a Fourth of July letter to a friend he repeated his remark to Crooks in 1822 that "candor is a leading trait in my character," and added an epitaph: ". . . though it has led to my official decapitation, I remain unchanged."[18]

The Senate Committee on Indian Affairs delayed seven weeks before finally reporting, on September 8, in favor of Mitchell's nomination. Five days later the Senate voted to confirm his appointment.[19] Dougherty and the Liberty Whigs opposed him because he was associated with Chouteau, but the *New Era* was "well satisfied" with him, and most St. Louis newspapers were relieved to have the conflict over, the office settled at last.[20] On September 21, Crawford formally notified Joshua of Mitchell's

[17] Ramsay Crooks to Pierre Chouteau, Jr., June 27, 1841, Chouteau MSS, MoSHi.

[18] Joshua Pilcher to John F. Darby, July 4, 1841, Darby Family Papers, MoSHi.; Second Auditor to Secretary of War Bell, June 29, and August 18, 1841, and to Joshua Pilcher, October 14, 1841, LB No. 28, pp. 19, 136, 213–14, Sec. A, USGAO, RG 217, NA.

[19] *Journal of the Senate*, V, 432, 440.

[20] *St. Louis New Era*, September 27, 1841.

appointment and asked him to give the new superintendent whatever information he needed on the job. Joshua, who knew the complexities of the position better than anyone else, anticipated Mitchell's problems and predicted, in a letter of August 20 to agent Cummins, regarding a claim against the government: ". . . [I] am very certain that it will be a long time before my successor can make himself sufficiently master of the subject to enable him to take any action in the case."[21] Joshua closed his accounts on September 5, but remained in Washington until October 18, a week after Mitchell filed his bond in St. Louis, before setting out for Missouri. He took the Baltimore and Ohio Railroad to Frederick, where he switched to a stage to Wheeling and, at the Ohio River, caught the steamboat *Effort* to Louisville and the *Messenger* from Louisville to St. Louis. The government paid for his transportation to and from Washington.[22]

Joshua landed in St. Louis on October 28. He was without a job for the first time in nearly ten years, but he had saved money while he was a federal officeholder and could afford to spend a leisurely fall and winter in St. Louis. He was proud of his record as an Indian agent and as superintendent—a century later the journalist-historian Bernard De Voto praised him as "one of a very few good agents" to the Indians—and enjoyed the companionship of many lifelong friends in St. Louis.[23] The city was recovering from the depression following the panic of 1837 and, in some ways, had changed little from the town Joshua first saw twenty-five years before. Quaint old wooden homes "with tumbledown galleries . . . queer little barbers' shops, and drinking houses"

[21] T. H. Crawford to Joshua Pilcher, September 21, 1841, LS, OIA, RG 75, NA; Joshua Pilcher to R. W. Cummins, August 20, 1841, Clark MSS, Vol. 7, p. 135, KHi.

[22] File 8143, RICC, RG 279, NA; Second Auditor to Lewis G. DeRussy[?], August 1, 1846, LB No. 35, pp. 427–28, Sec. A, USGAO, RG 217, NA; David D. Mitchell to D. Kurtz, October 12, 1841, LR, OIA, RG 75, NA.

[23] Bernard De Voto, *Across the Wide Missouri*, 295.

still lined the crooked, narrow streets near the levee, but "some very good houses . . . and marble-fronted shops" facing wide, straight streets in the newer part of town, set the pattern that the growing city followed when prosperity returned in the mid-forties.[24]

Early in November, Joshua sent his final accounts to the Indian Office. Unfortunately, they were incomplete, so, late in the month, he packed his bags, deposited $660 with Crooks in New York City, and once again returned to Washington. The government processed his accounts slowly. Nearly three months passed before he received word from the auditor, in March, 1842, that his vouchers had been examined and appeared to be correct. Although he was anxious to leave the East, he remained in Washington until May because he feared that he might be recalled to the capital if the second auditor discovered some small error in the accounts. Finally, late in the spring, he returned to St. Louis, but his accounts were not closed until May, 1843, a month before he died.[25]

While Joshua waited in Washington for the second auditor to examine his accounts, he repaired his political fences broken here and there by the prolonged battle over Keemle and Mitchell, and exchanged letters with friends in politics. In mid-April he congratulated George Maguire on his election as mayor of St. Louis and admonished him to "keep the ball in motion—the fall of 1844 will bring about an emense [sic] reduction in both the price & number of [Whigs] even in St. Louis."[26] He corresponded with Law-

[24] Charles Dickens, *American Notes for General Circulation and Pictures From Italy*, 204.

[25] Joshua Pilcher to T. H. Crawford, November 3, 1841, and May 4, 1842, LR, OIA, RG 75, NA; Pierre Chouteau, Jr., to Ramsay Crooks, No. 11817, November 27, 1841, American Fur Company Papers, NHi; Second Auditor to Joshua Pilcher, March 4, 1842, LB No. 29, p. 67, and May 8, 1843, LB No. 31, p. 55, Sec. A, USGAO, RG 217, NA.

[26] Joshua Pilcher to George Maguire, April 15, 1842, Pettus Family Papers, MoSHi.

rence Taliaferro about relations between Indians and land speculators in the upper Mississippi Valley, and in letters to Augustus C.
Dodge, Iowa's territorial delegate in Washington, he advanced
an opinion on the question of land claimed by the Sac and Foxes
between the Des Moines River and the northern boundary of
Missouri.[27] Late in April the Burlington *Gazette* published the
Dodge-Pilcher correspondence and endorsed Joshua's point of
view, expressed to Dodge, "that the Indian title has been fully
and fairly extinguished . . . that the right to the said tract is
exclusively vested in the United States; and that it is consequently
as much subject to occupation, survey and sale as any of the in-
habited parts of the territory." Joshua's opinion that the Sac and
Fox land south of the Des Moines River was open to settlement
added fuel to a major Iowa land controversy. Settlers immediately
poured into the Sac and Fox lands south of the Des Moines. Iowa
territorial officials complained bitterly to the Indian Office about
Joshua's interpretation of the law. Commissioner Crawford and
Secretary of War John C. Spencer denounced Joshua's statement
and reaffirmed the Sac and Fox claim to the land south of the
Des Moines. A few months later, however, in October, 1842, the
Sac and Foxes ceded to the United States their lands remaining in
Iowa and moved slowly to a reservation on the upper Osage River
in Kansas.[28]

Certainly, Joshua knew as well as anyone in the Indian service
that the Sac and Foxes did not give up all their Iowa land south of
the Des Moines River in the treaties of 1832 and 1837. Was he
simply carried away by his desire to see the Iowa frontier settled

[27] Joshua Pilcher to Lawrence Taliaferro, March 17, 1842, and to T. H.
Crawford, March 25, 1842, LR, OIA, RG 75, NA.

[28] Hagan, *Sac and Fox*, 220–23; John C. Spencer to John Calhoun, May 31,
1842, LS, Military Affairs, Records of the Office of the Secretary of War, RG
107, NA; John Chambers to T. H. Crawford, May 12 and June 21, 1842; O. H.
Stull to T. H. Crawford, May 7, 1842, and to John Beach, May 11, 1842; and
John Beach to O. H. Stull, May 9, 1842, LR, OIA, RG 75, NA.

and secured, against possible invasion from the north, in event of war with Britain over Oregon, or did he send Dodge his controversial opinion on the Sac and Fox claims to force the Indians to renew treaty negotiations, as Benton wished, before squatters overran their lands? Benton urged the administration to name Joshua to the treaty commission to negotiate the Iowa land issue, but Joshua's provocative statement on the Des Moines tract killed his chance to become a commissioner.[29]

He returned to Missouri during the height of the Sac and Fox controversy and settled down in St. Louis for the hot, unhealthy fever season, as Charles Dickens called summer in the Mississippi Valley.[30] In the middle of September Joshua became ill, and for two months Dr. James V. Prather treated him for a severe throat infection.[31] Unfortunately, he did not respond well to treatment and, in November, decided to go south to Cuba for the winter. To enable him to make the trip, Edward Brooks, Thomas Riddick's son-in-law who kept Joshua's accounts when Joshua was out of town, took up a note for $4,495.79 that Joshua had given Collier and Lindell of St. Louis, in November, 1836, to consolidate some of his debts. The note fell due in November, 1842, but Joshua was unable to meet it because Benton had failed to pay $3,800, also due in November, that he had borrowed from him.[32]

When the note was arranged satisfactorily, Joshua drew up a will, dated November 18, witnessed by Superintendent Mitchell and Howard F. Christy, leaving his estate to his closest living relative, his sister Margaret in Lexington—he did not mention his illegitimate son in Nebraska—and to close friends. He bequeathed $2,000 to Margaret; $500 in gold "American Eagles (Benton Money)" to his "faithfull friend" Haverty, who gave

[29] Alice Elizabeth Smith, *James Duane Doty*, 260–61.

[30] *American Notes*, 204.

[31] Voucher of Dr. James V. Prather in Estate of Joshua Pilcher, File No. 1803, St. Louis Probate Court, St. Louis, Missouri.

[32] Notes and Memoranda of Collier & Lindell and Thomas H. Benton in *ibid.*

him "eminent services" while he was Indian superintendent; his dueling pistols, valued at $30, to Benton's son John Randolph; his burial plot, appraised at $50.50, to Brooks; and Benton's note for $3,800 to the Senator to hold in trust for his daughter Susan until she became of suitable age to receive it. He left the residue of his estate to Thomas Riddick's widow, Eliza, and appointed Brooks administrator.[33]

Later in November, Joshua took a boat down the Mississippi to New Orleans where he booked passage on one of the schooners or brigs that sailed regularly from the Crescent City carrying passengers and cargo to Havana.[34] A few days later—five to eight days was normal sailing time—the vessel passed through the narrow, heavily fortified entrance to Havana harbor and anchored amidst dozens of other ships sheltered in the deep basin at the edge of the city. Joshua either rented a room in town—many of the boarding houses, however, were poor—or, more likely, accepted the hospitality of some American friend who lived in the city.[35] He spent four months in Cuba, enjoying the mild winter climate, but did not regain his health. In April he sailed for New Orleans with eleven other passengers aboard the brig *T. Street* laden with coffee, cigars, and tobacco. Five or six days later he disembarked at the first municipal pier in New Orleans, transferred his trunk to a riverboat, and returned home.[36]

[33] Will of Joshua Pilcher, November 18, 1842, in St. Louis Courthouse Papers, MoSHi. A copy of the will appears in Record of Wills C, pp. 83–84, St. Louis Probate Court, St. Louis, Missouri. Margaret Shaw died March 24, 1861 at the age of eighty-five. See the *Kentucky Statesman* (Lexington), March 26, 1861, for the announcement of her death.

[34] "Consular Returns. American Vessels Arriving at and Departing from the Port of Havana from the 21st of November, 1842 to the 1st of January, 1843," Despatches from United States Consuls in Havana, January 11, 1843–December 5, 1844, General Records of the Department of State, RG 59, NA.

[35] James Logan, *Notes of A Journey Through Canada, The United States of America, and the West Indies*, 198–201.

[36] Record of the Brig *T. Street*, Passenger Lists of Vessels Arriving at New

His illness, diagnosed as pulmonary consumption, worsened in St. Louis, and at the end of May he or his friends hired Jerry Cleaver, probably a Negro servant, to care for him.[37] On May 28 he added a codicil to his will to remove any ambiguity in his bequest to Susan Benton and, about the same time, gave a deposition in a case involving Chouteau.[38] Then, on May 29, he called in Brooks and "gave . . . [him] full directions respecting his interment" in the lot that he owned in Christ Church Episcopal Cemetery. He told Brooks that "whether he lived or died" he wanted the lot enclosed immediately by a fifteen-foot-square stone wall "sunk in the ground level with the surface," capped with stone, and surmounted with a three-foot heavy iron rail. He also directed Brooks to place "a thick stone level with the ground" over his grave and to raise over the gravestone, atop six marble pedestals, a slab of polished Italian marble bearing his name and place and dates of birth and death. Brooks immediately hired James Clark, a mason, to begin building the wall and contracted for the iron railing.[39]

Late in May or early in June, Joshua moved from his rather spartan living quarters to the comfortable mid-town home of a good friend, John Ruland, where he died on Monday evening,

---

Orleans, November 2, 1841–August 31, 1843, Records of the Bureau of Customs, RG 36, NA; *New-Orleans Commercial Bulletin*, April 24, 1843; *New-Orleans Bee*, April 24, 1843; *Daily Picayune* (New Orleans), April 25, 1843.

[37] Voucher of Jerry Cleaver in Estate of Joshua Pilcher, File No. 1803, St. Louis Probate Court, St. Louis; Register of Christ Church Cemetery, Entry of June 7, 1843, Christ Church Episcopal Cathedral, St. Louis.

[38] Codicil of May 28, 1843, Will of Joshua Pilcher, Record of Wills C, p. 84, St. Louis Probate Court, St. Louis; *Pierre Chouteau, Jr. v. Leonard Searcy* [?], November 11, 1843, Gamble Family Papers, MoSHi.

[39] Directions given by Joshua Pilcher respecting his cemetery lot and interment, and appended papers, St. Louis Courthouse Papers, MoSHi; Vouchers of James Clark in Estate of Joshua Pilcher, File No. 1803, St. Louis Probate Court, St. Louis.

June 5, 1843.[40] The *St. Louis New Era* and the *Daily Evening Gazette* printed short notices of his death, but the Democratic *Missouri Reporter* eulogized him for his Indian service and needled the "national administration" for firing him "solely on political grounds." The *Republican*, decidedly kinder to Joshua in death than in life, sent him "down to the tomb with an unsullied reputation, and the high esteem of many friends."[41]

Joshua was buried from Christ Church. Although he was not a communicant, he owned an Episcopal prayerbook, listed in the inventory of his estate, and may, on occasion, have attended services at Christ Church with members of the Riddick family. Brooks hired a dozen carriages to accommodate the mourners who accompanied the hearse from the church to Christ Church Cemetery in south St. Louis where Joshua was interred late in the afternoon of June 7.[42]

[40] *Daily Missouri Republican* (St. Louis), June 7, 1843.

[41] *Ibid.*; *St. Louis New Era*, June 6, 1843; *Daily Evening Gazette* (St. Louis), June 7, 1843; *Missouri Reporter* (St. Louis), June 8, 1843.

[42] *St. Louis New Era*, June 6, 1843; Register of Christ Church Cemetery, Entry of June 7, 1843, Christ Church Episcopal Cathedral, St. Louis; Vouchers of Robert O'Blenis, James Johnson, and James A. Thompson in Estate of Joshua Pilcher, File No. 1803, St. Louis Probate Court, St. Louis.

When Christ Church Cemetery was closed, Virginia C. Brooks, widow of Edward Brooks, authorized Joshua's remains to be removed to the Brooks plot in Bellefontaine Cemetery. See Transfer Permit No. 755 and note of V. C. Brooks, both dated April 21, 1884, in the Bellefontaine Cemetery Records, Bellefontaine Cemetery, St. Louis.

Brooks administered Joshua's estate fairly and honestly. On June 13 he inventoried the estate, in the presence of witnesses, and, on the following day, filed in court a preliminary appraisement of $12,459.41, later raised to $15,922.40. Joshua was frugal, and there is no documentary evidence that he ever accepted money from Chouteau or anyone else while serving as superintendent of Indian affairs.

Joshua owned only one piece of real property, his cemetery lot, and a small amount of personal property—clothes, a few pieces of furniture, some utensils, a pair of "gold spectacles," and "1 Black Trunk contg useless papers." He left the papers to Eliza Riddick who probably destroyed them. Today, of course, the papers would be called valuable historical manuscripts since they

173

The following day the *Missouri Reporter* eulogized Joshua as one of the "few men in the west . . . intimately acquainted with our Indian relations." No man was more "desirous" than Joshua Pilcher, the editor wrote, "of promoting the happiness and assuaging the miseries" of the red men. The editor used the right words, and Joshua, had he lived to read them, would have liked what they said.

---

doubtless documented in detail Joshua's career as a fur trader and public official. Most of the money in his estate was tied up in notes due him from borrowers or was held by Brooks on account. Brooks delivered Joshua's bequests to Margaret Shaw, John Haverty, Eliza Riddick, and the Bentons and took proper receipts in all cases. He also paid the debts allowed against the estate, including Joshua's note to Collier and Lindell, and settled court costs. In December, 1847, he filed final settlement on the estate and received his commission from the court. See the Estate of Joshua Pilcher, File No. 1803, St. Louis Probate Court, St. Louis.

I. Manuscripts

A. *Collections*

American Fur Company Ledgers K, W, X, Z, AA, BB, CC, DD, and EE, MoSHi.
American Fur Company Papers, NHi.
Bellefontaine Cemetery Records, Bellefontaine Cemetery, St. Louis.
Chouteau Family Papers, MoSHi.
Clark (William) Papers, Vols. 1, 4, 6, 7, 13, 18, 19, and 24, KHi.
Dougherty (John) Letter Book, 1826–29, MoHi.
Dougherty (John) Papers, MoSHi.
Fur Trade Papers, MoSHi.
Hempstead (Thomas) Letter Book (Missouri Fur Company), 1821–23, CtY-WA.
Jackson (Andrew) Papers (Microfilm of the Jackson Papers in the Library of Congress, Washington, D.C.), TSLA.
Kennerly (James) Diary, 1826–38, MoSHi.
Lisa (Manuel) Papers, MoSHi.
Lucas Family Papers, MoSHi.
Notes from Manuscripts Relating to the Omaha Indians, Mrs. Roy Green, Lincoln, Nebraska.
O'Fallon (Benjamin) Letter Book, 1823–29, CtY-WA.
Pilcher Family Genealogical Notes, Mrs. Margaret P. Vaughan, Alexandria, Virginia.
St. Louis Courthouse Papers, MoSHi.
Sappington Family Papers, MoSHi.

B. *Single Items*

Letters of:

Anonymous to Thomas(?) Forsyth, January 23, 1824, Forsyth Papers, Draper Collection of Manuscripts (Microfilm of the Draper Collection in the State Historical Society of Wisconsin), Rice Institute, Houston, Texas.

Joshua Pilcher to George Maguire, April 15, 1842, Pettus Family Papers, MoSHi.

Joshua Pilcher to John F. Darby, July 4, 1841, Darby Family Papers, MoSHi.

Joshua Pilcher to John Haverty, August 14, 1839, Indian Trade and Fur Companies Envelope, MoSHi.

Joshua Pilcher to Meredith M. Marmaduke, December 16, 1840, Marmaduke Papers, MoHi.

Lawrence Taliaferro to Joshua Pilcher, September 2, 1839, Taliaferro (Lawrence) Letter Book, Vol. 5 (1836–39), MnHi.

Thomas H. Benton to Joel R. Poinsett, n.d., Poinsett Papers, Historical Society of Pennsylvania, Philadelphia.

Thomas Hempstead to Joshua Pilcher, May 15, 1820, Hempstead Papers, MnHi.

Pierre Chouteau, Jr. v. Leonard Searcy(?), November 11, 1843, Gamble Family Papers, MoSHi.

Register of Christ Church Cemetery, Entry of June 7, 1843, Christ Church Episcopal Cathedral, St. Louis.

Shaw (Ralph) Typescript on the Shaw-Pilcher Families, MoSHi.

C. *Hudson's Bay Company Archives*

Material used in the text (drawn from the following manuscripts) is published by permission of the Governor and Committee of the Hudson's Bay Company. The PAC holds microfilm of the manuscripts.

Brandon House Post Journal, 1829–30, B.22/a/23.

Carlton House (Saskatchewan) Post Journal, 1829–30, B.27/a/18.
Cumberland House Account Book, 1829–30, B.49/d/27.
Cumberland House Post Journal, 1829–30, B.49/a/45.
Edmonton Account Book, 1829–30, B.60/d/33.
Jasper House Post Journal, 1829–30, B.94/a/2.
Winnipeg Post Journal, 1829–30, B.235/a/13.

II. Public Records

A. *United States Government Records in the National Archives*

Committee on Indian Affairs, Report No. 230 (Joshua Pilcher), January 27, 1836, Records of the United States House of Representatives, RG 233.

"Consular Returns. American Vessels Arriving at and Departing from the Port of Havana from the 21st of November, 1842 to the 1st of January, 1843," Despatches from United States Consuls in Havana, January 11, 1843–December 5, 1844, General Records of the Department of State, RG 59.

Fifth Census of the United States (1830), Fayette County, Kentucky, Record of the Bureau of the Census, RG 29.

Files 2761, 2778, 6317–A and B, and 20910, RICC, RG 279.

Fourth Census of the United States (1820), Fayette County, Kentucky, Records of the Bureau of the Census, RG 29.

Joel R. Poinsett to President Van Buren, February 24, 1841, and General Order No. 13, February 26, 1841, Records of the Adjutant General's Office, RG 94.

John C. Spencer to John Chambers, May 31, 1842, Letters Sent, Military Affairs, Records of the Office of the Secretary of War, RG 107.

Joshua Pilcher to Henry Clay, August 18, 1826, Letters Received, General Records of the Department of State, RG 59.

Letter Books Nos. 20, 23, 28, 29, 31, and 35, Sec. A, USGAO, RG 217.

Letters Received, 1824–43, OIA, RG 75.

Letters Sent, 1833–43, OIA, RG 75.

Passenger Lists of Vessels Arriving at New Orleans, November 2, 1841–August 31, 1843, Records of the Bureau of Customs, RG 36.

Registers of Letters Received by the Secretary of War, December 6 and 20, 1826, October, 1830–May, 1833, and July 10–14, 1841, RG 107.

Sixth Census of the United States (1840), Fayette County, Kentucky, Records of the Bureau of the Census, RG 29.

Tenth Census of the United States (1880), Soundex, Omaha Reservation, Nebraska, Records of the Bureau of the Census, RG 29.

B. *State Records*

Petition of the General Assembly from Citizens of Davidson County Respecting Negroes and Tipling Shops, 1813, Petitions and Memorials, Tenth General Assembly of the State of Tennessee, TSLA.

C. *County Records*

Circuit Court Record No. 2, 1819–23, Howard County Circuit Court, Fayette, Missouri.

Deed Record Book Q, Culpeper County Clerk's Office, Culpeper, Virginia.

Ed Pilcher v. *Fielding Pilcher*, 1821, Metal File Box 523–525, Fayette County Court, Lexington, Kentucky.

Estate of Edmond Shipp, File No. 252, St. Louis Probate Court, St. Louis, Missouri.

Estate of Joshua Pilcher, File No. 1803, St. Louis Probate Court, St. Louis, Missouri.

Execution Book, 1790–94, Culpeper County Clerk's Office, Culpeper, Virginia.

Executors Bonds No. 2, 1803–27, Fayette County Court, Lexington, Kentucky.

Joshua Pilcher v. *Joshua Norvell*, 1821–22, Metal File Box 529–531, Howard County Circuit Court, Fayette, Missouri.

Joshua Pilcher v. *Thompson Douglass*, Case Papers No. 182, August Term, 1819, St. Louis Circuit Court, St. Louis, Missouri.

Joshua Pilcher v. *William Grayson*, 1819, Metal File Box 176, Howard County Circuit Court, Fayette, Missouri.

Order Book 2, April, 1808–October, 1811, Fayette County Court, Lexington, Kentucky.

Personal Property Tax Lists for 1787–93, Culpeper County, Virginia, on deposit at the Virginia State Library, Richmond.

Record of Wills C, St. Louis Probate Court, St. Louis, Missouri.

Record 1, 1816–19, St. Louis Circuit Court, St. Louis, Missouri.

Tax List, 1811–12, Davidson County, Tennessee, on deposit at TSLA.

Tax List (Real Estate), 1824, St. Louis City Hall Archival Library, St. Louis, Missouri.

Tax Lists, 1796–1809, Fayette County, Kentucky, on deposit at the Kentucky Historical Society, Frankfort.

Will Book B, February, 1809–October, 1813, Fayette County Court, Lexington, Kentucky.

III. Government Publications

"A List of the Names of Persons Employed in the Indian Department during the Year 1836, and the Pay and Salary of Each," 24 Cong., 2 sess., *HED No. 141.*

"Abstract of Expenditures & Disbursements made by William Clark, October 1, 1831–September 30, 1832," 22 Cong., 2 sess., *HED No. 137.*

"Abstract of Licenses Granted to Persons to Trade in the Indian

Country. During the Year Ending 1st September, 1824," 18 Cong., 2 sess., *HD No. 54.*

"Abstract of Licenses Granted to Trade with the Indians," 19 Cong., 2 sess., *HD No. 86.*

Acts Passed By The General Assembly Of The Territory of Missouri; In December and January, One Thousand Eight Hundred and Sixteen and Seventeen. St. Louis, 1817.

American State Papers, II (Military Affairs). Washington, D.C., 1834.

"An Abstract of All Licenses Granted By Superintendencies of Indian Trade, & c. & c.," 18 Cong., 1 sess., *HD No. 7.*

"An Abstract of Licenses Granted to Citizens of the United States to Trade with the Indians During the Year ending 1 September, 1825," 19 Cong., 1 sess., *HD No. 118.*

"Indian Department—Persons Employed in 1839," 26 Cong., 1 sess., *HED No. 109.*

"Indians—Disbursement of Moneys, & c. For the Benefit of," 23 Cong., 1 sess., *HED No. 490.*

Journal of The Executive Proceedings of the Senate of the United States of America, III (1815–29), and V (1837–41). Washington, D.C., 1828 and 1887.

"Message From the President of the United States, In answer to a resolution of the Senate relative to the British establishments on the Columbia, and the state of the fur trade, & c," January 24, 1831, conaining Joshua Pilcher's Report to the Secretary of War, 21 Cong., 2 sess., *SD No. 39.*

"Message From the President of the United States, In Compliance with a Resolution of the Senate concerning the Fur Trade, and Inland Trade to Mexico," containing "Joshua Pilcher's Report" of December 1, 1831, "Mr. Pilcher's answers to queries relating to the Fur Trade, & c," a "Statement of the Location of posts for trade with the several Indian tribes within the Superintendency of Indian Affairs at St. Louis," and "A Tabular Statement showing the number of licenses issued to persons to trade with the Indians, in the years 1824, '5 '6, '7, '8, '9, '30, and '31; the amount of capital employed; with the value of the returns, as far as it can be ascertained," 22 Cong., 1 sess., *SD No. 90.*

"Mr. Pilcher's Answers to questions put to him by the Committee of the Senate on Indian Affairs," March 18, 1824, 18 Cong., 1 sess., *SD No. 56.*

Peters, Richard (ed.). *The Public Statutes at Large of the United States of America*, V, VI, and VII. Boston, 1856.

"Railroad To The Pacific Ocean," July 13, 1846, 29 Cong., 1 sess., *HR No. 773.*

"Report From the Secretary of War, with annual List of Officers and other persons engaged in the Indian Department," 24 Cong., 1 sess., *SD No. 109.*

Richardson, James D. (ed.). *A Compilation of the Messages and Papers of the Presidents 1789–1897*, II. Washington, D.C., 1898.

The Debates and Proceedings in the Congress of the United States (December 1, 1823–May 27, 1824). Washington, D.C., 1856.

IV. NEWSPAPERS

Boston Morning Post, October 28, 1837.

Daily Evening Gazette (St. Louis), June 6, 1840, June 4, 1841, and June 7, 1843.

Daily Evening Transcript (Boston), October 27 and 30, 1837.

Daily National Intelligencer (Washington, D.C.), January 17, 1832, September 18–October 25, 1837.

Daily Pennant and Native American (St. Louis), June 5, 1841.

Daily Picayune (New Orleans), April 25, 1843.

Democratic Clarion & Tennessee Gazette, or *Clarion & Tennessee State Gazette* (Nashville), September 24, 1811, March 8 and August 30, 1814.

Evening Post (New York City), October 25 and 26, 1837.

Independent Gazetteer (Lexington, Kentucky), March 8, 1805.

Kentucky Gazette (Lexington), November 7, 1799.

Kentucky Statesman (Lexington), March 26, 1861.

Maysville (Kentucky) *Eagle,* January 26, 1832.

Missouri Argus, or *St. Louis Argus,* June 4 and July 31, 1839, June 23 and 24, and July 25, 1840, and June 4, 1841.

Missouri Gazette (St. Louis), May 25 and August 17, 1816, March 22, October 4 and 11, and November 1 and 15, 1817, and February 20, March 6 and 13, and April 24, 1818.

Missouri Intelligencer (Franklin and Columbia), February 4, 1820, November 11, 18, and 25, and December 16, 1823, April 12, 1825, and July 21, 1832.

Missouri Reporter (St. Louis), June 8, 1843.

Missouri Republican, or *Daily Missouri Republican* (St. Louis), October 8 and 15, November 5 and 26, 1823, January 26, 1824, April 11, 1838, July 27, 1840, April 12, and June 4 and 7, 1841, and June 7, 1843.

Morning Courier and New-York Enquirer (New York City), October 23 and 25, 1837.

Morning Herald (New York City), October 26 and 27, 1837.

Nashville Whig, September 7, 1813, March 8, April 6, and October 25, 1814, and April 18, 1815.

National Gazette and Literary Register (Philadelphia), October 26, 1837.

New-Orleans Bee, April 24, 1843.

New-Orleans Commercial Bulletin, April 24, 1843.

New York Journal of Commerce (New York City), October 27, 1837.

New-York Spectator (New York City), October 26 and 30, 1837.

Pennsylvanian (Philadelphia), September 25, 1837.
Reporter (Lexington, Kentucky), October 21, 1809.
St. Louis Enquirer, October 18, 1823.
St. Louis New Era, June 4 and 6, 1840, June 4, 11, and 18, and
September 27, 1841, and June 6, 1843.
Sun (Baltimore), October 24, 1837.

V. Books

Abernethy, Thomas P. *From Frontier to Plantation in Tennessee.*
Chapel Hill, 1932.
Ardery, (Mrs.) William B. (comp.). *Kentucky Court and Other
Records*, II. Lexington, Kentucky, 1932.
Atherton, Lewis E. *The Pioneer Merchant in Mid-America (The
University of Missouri Studies*, Vol. XIV No. 2). Columbia,
Missouri, 1939.
Barker, Eugene C. (ed.). *The Austin Papers*, II. Washington,
D.C., 1922.
Bernhard, Duke of Saxe-Weimar Eisenach. *Travels Through
North America, During the Years 1825 and 1826.* Philadel-
phia, 1828.
Billon, Frederic L. *Annals of St. Louis in its Territorial Days
From 1804 to 1821.* St. Louis, 1888.
Bonner, T. D. *The Life and Adventures of James P. Beckwourth.*
Ed. by Bernard De Voto. New York, 1931.
Cable, John Ray. *The Bank of the State of Missouri (Columbia
University Studies in History, Economics and Public Law*, Vol.
CII No. 2). New York, 1923.
Chambers, William N. *Old Bullion Benton.* Boston and Toronto,
1956.
Chapman, Berlin B. *The Otoes and the Missourias.* Oklahoma
City, 1965.
Chittenden, Hiram M. *Early Steamboat Navigation on the Mis-*

souri River: Life and Adventures of Joseph La Barge, I. New York, 1903.

———. *The American Fur Trade of the Far West,* I. Palo Alto, 1954.

Clark, Thomas D. *A History of Kentucky.* New York, 1937.

Clift, G. Glenn. *Second Census of Kentucky—1800.* Frankfort, 1954.

———. *The "Corn Stalk" Militia of Kentucky 1792–1811.* Frankfort, 1957.

Collot, Victor. *A Journey in North America.* Trans. by J. Christian Bay. Florence, Italy, 1924.

Coman, Katharine. *Economic Beginnings of the Far West.* 2 vols. in 1. New York, 1930.

Cuming, F. *Sketches of a Tour Through the States of Ohio and Kentucky.* Ed. by Reuben G. Thwaites as Vol. IV of *Early Western Travels, 1748–1846.* Cleveland, 1904.

Decker, Peter (comp.). *A Descriptive Check List Together with Short Title Index Describing Almost 7500 Items of Western Americana...Formed by George W. Soliday.* New York, 1960.

Denslow, William R. *10,000 Famous Freemasons,* III (*Transactions of the Missouri Lodge of Research,* Vol. 14). Independence[?], Missouri, 1957.

De Voto, Bernard. *Across the Wide Missouri.* Boston, 1947.

Dickens, Charles. *American Notes for General Circulation and Pictures From Italy.* Philadelphia and London, n.d.

Douglas, Walter B. *Manuel Lisa.* Ed. by Abraham P. Nasatir. New York, 1964.

Ferrall, S. A. *A Ramble of Six Thousand Miles Through the United States of America.* London, 1832.

Frost, Donald McKay. *General Ashley: The Overland Trail And South Pass.* Barre, Massachusetts, 1960.

Garraghan, Gilbert J. *The Jesuits of the Middle United States,* I and II. New York, 1938.

Gray, William Henry. *A History of Oregon, 1792–1849.* Portland, 1870.

Grosart, Alexander B. (ed.). *The Poems and Literary Prose of Alexander Wilson, the American Ornithologist,* I. Paisley, England, 1876.

Hafen, LeRoy R., and Harlin M. Fuller. *The Journal of Captain John R. Bell (The Far West and the Rockie Historical Series,* Vol. 6). Glendale, California, 1957.

Hagan, William T. *The Sac and Fox Indians.* Norman, Oklahoma, 1958.

Hulbert, Archer Butler, and Dorothy P. *Marcus Whitman, Crusader, Part One, 1802 to 1839 (Overland to the Pacific,* Vol. 9). Denver and Colorado Springs, 1936.

James, Edwin. *Account of an Expedition from Pittsburgh to the Rocky Mountains, Performed in the Years 1819, 1820.* Ed. by Reuben G. Thwaites as Vol. XIV of *Early Western Travels, 1748–1846.* Cleveland, 1905.

Jennings, Marietta. *A Pioneer Merchant of St. Louis 1810–1820 (Columbia University Studies in History, Economics, and Public Law,* No. 462). New York, 1939.

Lavender, David. *Bent's Fort.* New York, 1954.

Logan, James. *Notes of A Journey Through Canada, The United States of America, and the West Indies.* Edinburgh, London, and Dublin, 1838.

McRaven, William Henry. *Nashville, "Athens of the South."* Chapel Hill, 1949.

Marryat, Frederick. *Diary in America.* Ed. by Jules Zanger. Bloomington, Indiana, 1960.

Maximilian, Prince of Wied. *Travels in the Interior of North America.* Ed. by Reuben G. Thwaites as Vols. XXII, XXIII, and XXIV of *Early Western Travels, 1748–1846.* Cleveland, 1906.

Meigs, William M. *The Life of Thomas Hart Benton*. Philadelphia and London, 1904.

Melish, John. *Travels Through The United States of America, in the Years 1806 & 1807, and 1809, 1810, & 1811*. Philadelphia and Belfast, 1818.

Merk, Frederick. *Fur Trade and Empire (Harvard Historical Studies*, Vol. XXXI). Cambridge and London, 1931.

Michaux, François A. *Travels to the West of the Alleghany Mountains, in the States of Ohio, Kentucky, and Tennessee*. Ed. by Reuben G. Thwaites as Vol. III of *Early Western Travels, 1748–1846*. Cleveland, 1904.

Morgan, Dale L. *Jedediah Smith and the Opening of the West*. Boston, 1953.

———. (ed.), *The West of William H. Ashley*. Denver, 1964.

———, and Eleanor Towles Harris (eds.). *The Rocky Mountain Journals of William Marshall Anderson*. San Marino, California, 1967.

Morton, J. Sterling. *Illustrated History of Nebraska*, I. Lincoln, 1911.

Oglesby, Richard E. *Manuel Lisa and the Opening of the Missouri Fur Trade*. Norman, 1963.

Phillips, Paul C. *The Fur Trade*, II. Norman, 1961.

Pilcher, Lewis S. *A Surgical Pilgrim's Progress*. Philadelphia and London, 1925.

Pilcher, Margaret Campbell. *Historical Sketches of the Campbell, Pilcher, and Kindred Families*. Nashville, 1911.

Pusey, William A. *The Wilderness Road to Kentucky*. New York, 1921.

Rich, E. E. (ed.). *Part of Dispatch From George Simpson Esqr Governor of Rupert's Land to the Governor and Committee of the Hudson's Bay Company London March 1, 1829. Continued and Completed March 24 and June 5, 1829 (The Publi-*

cations of the Hudson's Bay Record Society, 10). Toronto, 1947.

———, (ed.). *The Letters of John McLoughlin From Fort Vancouver to the Governor and Committee First Series, 1825–38 (The Publications of the Hudson's Bay Records Society*, 4). Toronto, 1941.

Royall, Anne. *Letters from Alabama on Various Subjects.* Washington, D.C., 1830.

Saum, Lewis O. *The Fur Trader and The Indian.* Seattle and London, 1965.

Schoolcraft, Henry R. *The Indian in His Wigwam.* Buffalo, 1848.

Sealsfield, Charles. *The Americans as They Are.* London, 1828.

Shambaugh, Benjamin F. (ed.). *Executive Journal of Iowa 1838–1841.* Iowa City, 1906.

Smith, Alice Elizabeth. *James Duane Doty.* Madison, Wisconsin, 1954.

Smith, Elbert B. *Magnificent Missourian: The Life of Thomas Hart Benton.* Philadelphia and New York, 1958.

Snodgrass, Charles A. *The History of Freemasonry in Tennessee, 1789–1943.* Chattanooga, 1944.

Staples, Charles R. *The History of Pioneer Lexington (Kentucky) 1779–1806.* Lexington, 1939.

Steiner, James B. *History of Missouri Lodge No. 1 (Transactions of the Missouri Lodge of Research*, Vol. 2). St. Louis[?], 1944.

Stuart, James. *Three Years in North America*, II. Edinburgh, 1833.

Toulmin, Harry. *The Western Country In 1793.* Ed. by Marion Tinling and Godfrey Davies. San Marino, California, 1948.

Young, F. G. (ed.). *The Correspondence and Journals of Captain Nathaniel J. Wyeth 1831–6 (Sources of the History of Oregon*, Vol. I). Eugene, 1899.

VI. Articles

Allis, Samuel. "Forty Years among the Indians and on the Eastern Borders of Nebraska," *Transactions and Reports of the Nebraska Historical Society*, Vol. II (1887), 133–66.

Bradford, John E. (ed.). "The James McBride Manuscripts," *Quarterly Publication of the Historical and Philosophical Society of Ohio*, Vol. V (January–March, 1910), 21–31.

Buck, Solon J. (ed.). "Pioneer Letters of Gershom Flagg," *Transactions of the Illinois State Historical Society For the Year 1910*, 139–83.

"Death of Mrs. John Pilcher." *Nebraska History*, Vol. V (July, 1922), 49.

DeLand, Charles E., and Doane Robinson. "Fort Tecumseh and Fort Pierre Journal and Letter Books," *South Dakota Historical Collections*, Vol. IX (1918), 69–239.

Dyer, L. C. "The Early Days of Freemasonry in Missouri," *The Missouri Freemason*, September 27, 1913.

Ernst, Ferdinand. "Travels In Illinois In 1819," *Transactions of the Illinois State Historical Society For the Year 1903*, 150–65. 1956), 2–11.

Ewers, John C. "When The Light Shone in Washington," *Montana, the Magazine of Western History*, Vol. VI (October,

"Extracts from the Diary of Rev. Moses Merrill, a Missionary to the Otoe Indians from 1832 to 1840," *Transactions and Reports of the Nebraska Historical Society*, Vol. IV (1892), 160–91.

Gallaher, Ruth A. "Indian Agents in Iowa," *The Iowa Journal of History and Politics*, Vol. XIV (July, 1916), 348–94.

Gronert, Theodore G. "Trade in the Blue-Grass Region, 1810–1820," *Mississippi Valley Historical Review*, Vol. V (December, 1918), 312–23.

Hulbert, Archer B. (ed.). "The First Wagon Train on the Road to Oregon," *The Frontier*, Vol. X (January, 1930), 147–68.

"Indian Affairs of Iowa in 1840," *Annals of Iowa*, Vol. XV (April, 1926), 255–80.

Jensen, (Mrs.) Dana O. "The Enigma of Mr. Shaw," *The Bulletin of the Missouri Historical Society*, Vol. XV (July, 1959), 310–18.

Missouri Grand Lodge Bulletin, Vol. 4 (November, 1927), 167.

Nasatir, Abraham P. "The International Significance of the Jones and Immell Massacre and of the Aricara Outbreak of 1823," *The Pacific Northwest Quarterly*, Vol. XXX (January, 1939), 77–108.

Newmill, P. M. "Stephen F. Austin, Duelist," *Bunker's Magazine*, Vol. I (January, 1928), 47–56.

North American Review, Vol. CVI (January, 1840), 75–144.

Paul Wilhelm, Duke of Wuerttemberg. "First Journey to North America in the Years 1822 to 1824," in William G. Bek (ed. and trans.), *South Dakota Historical Collections*, Vol. XIX (1938), 1–474.

Peterson, Charles E. "Manuel Lisa's Warehouse," *The Bulletin of the Missouri Historical Society*, Vol. IV (January, 1948), 59–91.

Phillips, Paul C. "William Henry Vanderburgh: Fur Trader," *Mississippi Valley Historical Review*, Vol. XXX (December, 1943), 377–94.

Pilcher, Harriet L. "My Pioneer Life In Nebraska," N. p., n. d.

Quisenberry, A. C. (ed.). " 'Heads of Families' in Fayette County, Census of 1810," *The Register of the Kentucky State Historical Society*, Vol. XX (May, 1922), 145–69.

Reid, Russell, and Clell G. Gannon (eds.). "Journal of the Atkinson-O'Fallon Expedition," *North Dakota Historical Quarterly*, Vol. IV (October, 1929), 1–56.

Robinson, Doane (ed.). "Official Correspondence Pertaining to the Leavenworth Expedition of 1823 into South Dakota For the Conquest of the Ree Indians," *South Dakota Historical Collections*, Vol. I (1902), 181–256.

Stauf, Margaret. "John Dougherty, Indian Agent," *Mid-America*, Vol. XVI (January, 1934), 135–46.

"The Journal of Needham Parry—1794," *The Register of the Kentucky State Historical Society*, Vol. XXXIV (October, 1936), 378–91.

Wesley, Edgar B. "Diary of James Kennerly 1823–1826," *Missouri Historical Society Collections*, Vol. VI (October, 1928), 41–97.

White, James Haley. "Early Days in St. Louis," *Glimpses of the Past*, Vol. VI (January–March, 1939), 5–30.

Williams, Samuel C. "Nashville As Seen By Travelers, 1801–1821," *Tennessee Historical Magazine*, Series II, Vol. I (April, 1931), 182–206.

VII. Essays

Oglesby, Richard E. "The Fur Trade as Business," 111–27, in John F. McDermott (ed.). *The Frontier Re-examined*. Urbana, Chicago, and London, 1967.

Arikara Indians, 38; visits Mandan Indians and supervises construction of Fort Vanderburgh, 38–39; attacked by Arikara Indians, 39; learns of Blackfoot ambush, 40; recalls traders from Northwest, 41; and difficulties of Missouri Fur Company, 41; hears of attack by Arikara Indians, 43; accompanies Army expedition against Arikaras, 43–48; complimented by Gen. Leavenworth, 45; injured in battle, 47; criticized for handling of Indians, 48–49; and controversy over Arikara campaign, 50–54, 56, 59; writes letter attacking Col. Leavenworth, 51; reports on fur trade to U.S. Senate Committee on Indian Affairs, 53–54; orders Fort Vanderburgh destroyed, 54; entertains Prince Paul Wilhelm, Duke of Wuerttemberg, 54–55; sends traders to Wyoming, 55; visits Washington, D.C., 56; orders Fort Recovery abandoned, 57–58; dissolves Missouri Fur Company, 59; reopens trade with Indians, 59–60; appointed U.S. consul at Chihuahua, Mexico, 60–61; forms Joshua Pilcher and Company, 61–63; assumes debts of Missouri Fur Company, 64; resigns as consul to Chihuahua, 64; competes for fur trade, 64–65; abandons Missouri River trade, 66; leaves for Rocky Mountains, 66–68; and failure of Joshua Pilcher and Company, 69; offers services to Hudson's Bay Company, 70–71; travels through Canada, 72–78; returns to St. Louis, 79; reports on journey to U.S. Senate, 80–83; reports on fur trade to U.S.

War Department, 84–87; visits Washington, D.C., 88; appointed agent to Sac and Fox Indians (Rock Island, Ill.), 89–90; works to end Black Hawk War, 91–92; and Indian annuities controversy, 93–96; criticizes John Dougherty, Upper Missouri agent, 96–98; criticizes federal Indian policy, 97–98; works for American Fur Company, 98–99; supervises agency at Council Bluffs, Iowa, 100–11; entertains Prince of Wied-Neuwied, 101–104; described by Samuel Allis, 104–105; and cholera epidemic, 105–106; marries half-blood Omaha Indian, 107; son of, 107–108; appointed Sioux sub-agent at Fort Lookout, 110; and Indian annuities, 111–12; reports on Sioux sub-agency, 115; visits tribes of sub-agency, 117; investigates other traders for American Fur Company, 117–18; attends rendezvous of 1836, 118–19; described by missionaries, 118 & n.; advises Dr. Marcus Whitman about Indians, 119; helps negotiate Platte Purchase, 120–21; as Indian agent to Sioux, Cheyenne, and Ponca Indians, 122–40; and smallpox epidemic, 123–25; escorts delegation of Indians on tour of East, 124–33; and Indian council in Washington, D.C., 127–30; concludes treaty with Ioway Indians, 133; on Indian annuity payments, 134–35; on Indian trade, 136 & n.; moves agency to Vermillion River, 136–37, 140; and smallpox epidemic, 137–40; assigned Mandan Sub-Agency, 137; appointed superintendent of Indian

Stewart, Sir William Drummond: 118, 119

Stone, Bostwick and Company: 31, 34

Street, Gen. Joseph M.: 130, 157

Stuyvesant Institute (New York City): 131

Sublette, Andrew: 117n.

Sublette, Milton: 117 & n.

Sublette, Pinckney: 117n.

Sublette, Solomon: 117n.

Sublette, William L.: 67, 72, 80, 109, 117n.

Sublette and Campbell: 117

Superintendency of Indian Affairs at St. Louis: 141–61; *see also* William Clark, Joshua Pilcher, Jr.

Sweetwater River: 68

Swift Run Gap (Blue Ridge): 5

Taliaferro, Lawrence: 148, 168–69

Tennessee, state of: 5, 12, 17

Tennessee Volunteers (War of 1812): 15

Teton River: 44, 78

Teton Sioux: 139; *see also* Sioux Indians

Texas: 21

Thornton River: 3

Three Forks (Missouri River): 40

Transylvania University (Lexington, Ky.): 10, 21

Treaty of Ghent: 18

Treaty of Prairie du Chien: 97, 133

T. Street (brig): 171

Tyler, Pres. John: 161, 165, 166

U.S. Army: 29, 36, 44, 52, 128; expedition of, against Arikara Indians, 43–48

U.S. Circuit Court (St. Louis, Mo.): 26

U.S. Congress: 32, 84, 85, 110, 114, 129, 135, 162–63

U.S. House of Representatives: 53, 62, 83, 88, 89; Committee of Indian Affairs, 53, 89, 114

U.S. Indian Office: 79, 84, 88ff., 92, 95ff., 111ff., 116–17, 119, 122ff., 125, 129ff., 134–36, 142ff., 147–49, 151–53, 155, 158, 161, 162, 165ff.; reorganized by Congress, 1834, 110; appoints Pilcher Superintendent of Indian Affairs at St. Louis, 141–43; *see also* T. Hartley Crawford, Carey A. Harris, Elbert Herring

U.S. Senate: 9, 32, 80, 95, 96; Committee on Indian Affairs, 53, 122, 143, 166; report to, from Joshua Pilcher, 80–83; prints Pilcher's report on fur trade, 86–87

U.S. State Department: 64

U.S. War Department: 56, 110, 114, 128, 141; *see also* John Bell, Lewis Cass, Joel R. Poinsett, U.S. Indian Office

Upper Missouri Indian Agency (Fort Lookout, Big Bend): 85, 96–97, 129; Pilcher appointed to, 122–40; and smallpox epidemic, 123–25; moved to Vermillion River, 136–37, 140, 142, 145

Van Buren, Pres. Martin: 122, 127–28, 130, 135, 141–43, 150, 159–60, 162, 163

Vanderburgh, William Henry: 30, 37–39, 44, 61–64, 69

Vermillion River: 115, 116, 119, 137

Vermont, state of: 53

Virginia, state of: 3–8

Wales, England: 4

The text for *Joshua Pilcher: Fur Trader and Indian Agent* has been set on the Linotype in 11½-point Caslon, a faithful rendering of an original type designed by William Caslon. The book is printed on special paper bearing the watermark of the University of Oklahoma Press and is designed to have an effective life of at least three hundred years.